IN
YOUR
HANDS

Your child is in your hands! A responsibility? . . .Yes! A rare privilege, too!

IN YOUR HANDS

*The Parents
Guide Book*

The United Educators, Inc.
LAKE BLUFF, ILLINOIS
1997

Acknowledgements and photo credits will be found at the end of this book

You Are Your Child's First Teacher

THE CHILD'S FIRST TEACHERS are his parents. From the moment of birth, the infant's father and mother are devoted to protecting the life and health of their child. During infancy, his efforts in communication, his spiritual growth, and his play activities are also guided by his parents. As the months and years of infancy advance, the child shares with his parents these responsibilities. By the time he is old enough to enter kindergarten, his parents have taught him to feed and dress himself, to listen to stories, to meet toilet needs, to follow safety rules, and to be a participating member of the family. This great beginning in the child's education shows the *parents truly to be teachers.**

All parents are teachers, the all but indispensable teachers. And as teachers, parents always have had the first and largest responsibility for educating their children. . . . The fact that we have established public schools is not a surrender by parents of their basic responsibility for education. Each parent still has that responsibility.†

* The Preschool Curriculum of the Chicago Public Schools.
† David Guterson. *Family Matters: Why Homeschooling makes Sense* (page 16).
© 1992 by David Guterson. A Harvest Book, Harcourt Brace & Company.

What do you

dream of for

your child?

Security

Happiness

Success

Goodness

"Few things are more right than a child's mind when we first come in contact with it. What it later becomes is <u>our responsibility</u>."

Contributors and Advisers

EVERETT EDGAR SENTMAN
B.S., University of Illinois, Drake University, Loyola University,
    American Conservatory

JACQUES BARZUN
Professor Emeritus
Columbia University

BERNICE E. CULLINAN
Reading Specialist
Professor of Early Childhood and Elementary Education
New York University

MARTHA BENNETT KING
B.A., University of Chicago
Director, The *Chicago Tribune* Miracle of Books
Author, *Growth of American Family in History*

MARGARET ROHNER LINDMAN
M.A., Northwestern University
Ed.D., Loyola University
Associate Professor of Education, Northeastern Illinois State College
Tangley Oaks Advisory Editor

RALPH K. MEISTER
Ph.D., University of Chicago
Director, Clinic for Child Guidance, Mooseheart, Illinois

OLIVE BEAUPRÉ MILLER
B.L., Smith College
Editor in Chief Emeritus, *My Book House*

EDWIN C. REICHERT
Ph.D., University of Minnesota
Chairman, Department of Education, Lake Forest College
Coauthor, *Time to Read Elementary Readers*

MARTIN L. REYMERT
Founder and for many years Director
The Mooseheart Laboratory for Child Research

Table of Contents

Preface

In Your Hands is designed to aid *My Book House* parents in an effective use of the age-graded material in *My Book House Plan* and to act as a guide to successful parenthood. The direct relationship between the material and the needs and interests of your growing child is made clear.

Since most parents have never had an opportunity to learn the stages through which children develop normally, they may need expert help if they are to guide their child's day-to-day progress with wisdom and understanding. The purpose of Home-School Coordinating Charts, chapter 15, and chapter 16, Climbing the Ladder of Years, is to provide this help. Both are based on data obtained from observation, tests, and school courses of study. The standards set up for the average child at each level are not absolute requirements for any individual child. They simply indicate the stages of development through which each child is expected to grow at *his or her own rate.*

Many of the problems that develop between parents and their child come from the fact that too much is expected too soon. There are two important things for parents to know if they are really to understand their growing boys and girls: (1) the general or average pattern and rate at which all children grow and (2) the individual child's own pattern and rate of growing.

Throughout *In Your Hands* we provide authoritative information on the subject of child development and a guide for parents in understanding and helping their child.

IN
YOUR
HANDS

*A*ll parents are teachers, the all but indispensable teachers.

1

Your Child
Is In Your Hands

Many parents are intimidated when they first read this challenging statement and realize the responsibility it places on them in affecting the success and happiness of their child.

It was to help the thousands of parents who have difficulty finding the material they need to guide their child's development that *My Book House Plan* was developed. With this plan as a guide you will feel confident that you are using, in your own home, the simple, practical findings of years of research in the field of child study. It will place at your fingertips a guide for understanding many aspects of child development and provide practical answers to your questions about your child's development *before* they arise. Knowing the best thing to do at the best time will help eliminate fear, uncertainty, and emotional upsets in the child's day. Above all, it will prepare you to meet your child's needs and secure your child's happy cooperation.

You will find an everyday use for this plan in your home, and the understanding you gain from this daily contact with the things that go to make up your child's world will help you be more sympathetic and understanding in your relationship with him.

The Well-Balanced Child Is the Happy Child

Above everything else, you want your child to develop into a happy, alert, and well-balanced individual. The mental diet you select for your child greatly affects his thoughts and actions and helps shape his personality. A child's mental development depends on a well-balanced mental diet in much the same way his physical development depends on wholesome and nourishing food. The conversations your child hears, the experiences he has, the stories and rhymes you read to him are all part of his mental diet.

My Book House Plan gives your child a choice mental diet that will encourage the development of wonderful qualities. The plan will increase your confidence because it will help you meet the many phases of their development with intelligence and understanding. No "outside the home" training will ever replace the influence of story time in your own home. Children unconsciously pattern their ideals after the thoughts and actions of the people they admire. Your child will be challenged by the truth, honesty, courage, and adventures of the characters in the stories you read to him. Here, in *My Book House,* your child will become familiar with some of the world's finest literature and learn to sense its beauty and appeal. The selections will attract and interest him and offer him patterns for living.

Preparation for Adolescence Begins at Birth

Having a feeling of security, of being loved and understood, will do much to guide your child safely and happily through his whole life.

Building a child's confidence and trust is a day-to-day process and should begin at birth. Following *My Book House Plan* will keep you in close contact with your child as he matures and develops and will serve as a guidepost to you in offering intelligent and sympathetic guidance. Your willingness to get into your child's world and understand the developmental tasks he must master will earn his confidence. The inner security gained in this way will help your child deal with some common problems that may come with adolescence.

Three Services in My Book House Plan

The twelve beautifully illustrated volumes of *My Book House* form the basis of the three services the complete *My Book House Plan* brings to your home. The understanding and close companionship that will result from the use of this material will more than repay you for the little time you spend each day unfolding it with your child.

Part 1 of the plan is represented by the twelve carefully selected and age-graded volumes of *My Book House,* which include 2,772 pages of age-graded selections from over fifty different countries. There are over 2,000 illustrations, more than half of which are in full color. The extensive index, found in volume XII, will prove invaluable to you in choosing the right material for your child's interests at each stage of his development. Character qualities such as confidence, courage, truthfulness, perseverance, and many others that you will want to encourage in your child are found in the Character Building Index. Under each quality of character are listed selections to help build specific qualities in your child.

Part 2 is this book, the new *In Your Hands.* It covers substantially every phase of your child's development from infancy through adolescence. Your attention is focused on the important aspects of your child's mental, emotional, and social development, and reference is made to helpful material in *My Book House*. The table of contents of this book, with its chapter summaries, will enable you to quickly locate the material you need, as you need it. You will find it worthwhile to examine the table of contents before you introduce your child to *My Book House*.

Part 3 of *My Book House Plan* is *Your Child's World*. Written by many specialists, this book brings you numerous brief, easy-to-use articles, the specific answers to daily training questions. Moreover, a number of these articles are in an entertaining and thought-provoking quiz form.

A child is like a piece of living clay.

You touch and mold it day by day.

The only one who can truly mold character

and shape his future is

YOU!

*H*old your
baby on your lap
while you read
to her.

2

Appreciation of Literature Begins Early

Research on families of early readers shows some common characteristics in materials, activities, and attitudes. *In Your Hands* provides detailed information and suggestions as to how to achieve these conditions, but first we will have a brief overview. In terms of materials, parents should have reading materials available for children which *My Book House* goes a long way toward accomplishing. The parent might also want to supplement this by intriguing children with new and different books on a regular basis. This can be easily accomplished by using your local public library. It is also suggested that you place, as your child grows older, some of her books, as well as your own books, magazines, and newspapers, throughout the house in order to promote spontaneous reading. In addition, providing materials that encourage writing, such as pens, pencils, and crayons, as well as materials that let her create her own stories, such as puppets and dolls, will further help your child appreciate reading.

Activities that help promote early literacy include reading to your child on a daily basis and talking about the stories; encouraging her to read along

with you when she is able; encouraging telling stories to each other; talking to your child about the things you have read; pointing out printed materials in your daily environment, such as that on signs or cereal boxes; and finally, being a role model for your child by reading and writing for yourself.

Attitudes that help early reading grow include praising your child's attempts at reading and writing; answering her questions about reading and writing; and encouraging reading and writing as pleasurable experiences so your child will come to associate them with enjoyment.

During the first two years of life, children are very busy investigating the many new things they are discovering in the world around them. Children are constantly learning using all of their senses. During these early days, then, is the time to lay the foundation for the appreciation of literature and the enjoyment of reading in your child.

Infants enjoy pleasant sounds from the time they are a few weeks old. The regular accenting of certain syllables of the nursery rhymes and stories you read to them are a joy long before words assume meaning. Indeed, in newborns the sense of hearing is more developed than sight. Unconsciously, children's growing sense of rhythm makes it easier for them to time their movements and develop confidence. Their actions and speech are influenced by their feeling for rhythm. Indeed, some research indicates that infants breathe rhythmically to language. Love of modulated sounds may later flower into an appreciation of poetry and music.

Since the infant's hearing is active from birth, the very sound of parental voices will carry messages long before words become meaningful. If the earliest voices heard are rhythmical and pleasing, they will carry a message of love and security. Parents who sing lullabies and repeat nursery rhymes are influencing their child far more than is realized. Infants learn to identify some of the voices they hear every day. Psychologists tell us that we must first learn to listen before we are ready to listen to learn. The mother and father who sing and play rhymes with their baby encourage listening and paying attention right from the beginning.

Introducing Your Baby to My Book House.

We suggest holding your baby on your lap while you read to her. It is only natural that a baby will want to examine the colorful pictures she sees before her. Be sure to give your baby the opportunity to satisfy her curiosity before you begin reading. Placing your finger under the picture that tells about the rhyme you are reading may help hold her attention. It will also help your baby connect the sound and meaning of the words she hears with the pictures she sees.

A little planning on your part will give your baby a pleasant introduction to books and literature. When you first begin reading your baby may listen for only a few brief moments, as children's attention spans are short at this age. If you notice she is becoming restless, it is wise to stop, close the book carefully, and carry the baby with you as you return the book to the shelf. The next day, preferably at the same time, bring that book from the shelf and begin to read to her in much the same manner as you did the day before. Following this very simple procedure with regularity, a few minutes each day, will help your baby form the habit of listening and looking attentively. The period following your baby's bath is usually a very good time for reading. Soon your baby will look forward to story time with you, and she

will gradually want to look and listen for longer periods of time. By the end of the first year, you will have helped her form the important habit of listening and concentrating.

Baby Reflects Your Attitude Toward Books

Your child quickly senses your attitude and actions toward books as well as other things.

You will find your child will imitate how you handle books. If, for example, when you turn a page, you take the time to carefully lift the upper right hand corner of it, and say slowly and rhythmically, "o—ver," your child will come to associate the word *over* with turning pages. As soon as your child is old enough, let *her* turn the pages of her books. If, in reaching for it, an accident occurs and a page becomes torn or soiled, do not be disturbed and, above all, don't scold them. You want your child to feel comfortable with their books, to regard them with affection, and to feel a certain amount of freedom in handling them. Try to see that your and your child's hands are clean before handling the books and try to impart to her the attitude that books are possessions to be cherished. There is great significance in the title *My Book House*. By the time your child is ready to enter kindergarten or first grade, you will have helped her discover the joy of reading and encouraged an eagerness to learn to read better in order to enjoy more stories.

In the first two volumes of *My Book House*, you will find beautifully illustrated lullabies and rhymes gathered from twenty-nine countries. These include Mother Goose, the folk rhymes of America, and simple poems by such authors as Shakespeare, Keats, Tennyson, Rossetti, and Stevenson. Also included in these two volumes are simple activities and repetitive stories that will interest your baby. By making full use of the three-part comprehensive index in volume XII of *My Book House*, you will become more familiar with the fine heritage of children's literature. Parents familiar with fine children's literature are well equipped to kindle and nurture the appreciation of literature in their child. For more information, see the language development and literature activities in the various charts in chapter 15 of this book.

*Raising Readers**

By Bernice E. Cullinan

RAISING CHILDREN is one of the most important jobs you'll ever tackle. You didn't apply for the job; you don't get paid one cent to do it; it's a twenty-four-hour-a-day job; you don't get vacations from it; and it lasts for many years. The job—being a parent—has a great payoff.

Although you aren't paid in money, the rewards are tremendous. The rewards come from watching your children grow into loving, responsible, competent human beings. That's no small accomplishment! Our children are the hope of the future. We need to nurture them carefully. If you teach your children to love to read, you are handing down a special kind of magic to them—a gift that will enrich their lives as nothing else can do.

You take your job seriously. You make sure your child eats healthy food and has proper rest. You get sneakers that are the right size so the feet will grow straight. You buy the right kind of clothes to make sure your child stays warm. But what about your child's mind—are you feeding the imagination? Are you feeding that endless curiosity that causes children's minds to grow in a healthy way?

It seems as if you answer a hundred of your child's questions a day and you know you will continue to answer lots more. But you also know that your child needs to learn from other sources, too—and that includes books! Books contain an endless source of knowledge . . . and pleasure . . . .

You may say, "But I don't know how to teach my child to be a reader. That's the school's job." Certainly the school has a very important role to play and will spend many years developing reading skills, but you have the most important, most continuous, and most lasting influence on your child

---

*Excerpt from Bernice E. Cullinan. "Raising Readers" in *Read to Me: Raising Kids Who Love to Read* (pages 5–7). © 1992 by Bernice E. Cullinan. Reprinted by permission of Scholastic Inc.

as a reader! The school needs you as a partner; your continued support over the years makes a lasting difference. School cannot do the job alone nor can school do it as well as it could with your help.

Some very simple things you do now have a big payoff in the years to come. For example, you can say, "Come here and look at this book I'm reading. It's about books I'm supposed to read to you. Let's see if we can find one that looks good to you." Letting your children know that you are interested in their books tells them that reading is important to you. Even more crucial, it tells them that they are important to you. Asking them to find books they like shows that you want them to enjoy reading; it tells them reading is not a chore, but something you are supposed to enjoy. It is the beginning of many happy hours spent sharing books.

A baby's vocabulary truly begins the moment he hears his first word spoken.

3

Language Development Begins at Birth

YOUR CHILD'S ABILITY to use and understand language will affect many aspects of his development. It plays a very important role in his mental growth and helps him adjust to new situations and people.

A baby's vocabulary truly begins the moment he hears a word spoken. Parents talk and sing to babies for months with no expectation that they will immediately use the language they hear. By the process of constant repetition children begin to understand and later reproduce words. Children have a listening, understanding, and speaking vocabulary long before they learn to read, write, and spell words.

Speech Habits Formed Early

Since children learn to use language by imitating and listening to parents, you should expose your child to good speech from the very beginning. Baby talk and talking down to a child may hamper his desire and ability to use language. Children develop language ability very rapidly during their preschool years, and the style of their speech reflects their early home speaking environment. Educators agree that the conditions most likely to affect a child's language development are those prevailing in his own home, long before he enters school.

And, remember, children must be able to hear well to be able to make distinctions between similar sounds. Middle ear infections and physical hearing impairments can affect your child's ability to hear and thus learn language and communicate. It is important to watch your child to make sure he is hearing well and to have his hearing checked by a physician if you suspect there is a problem. You should also make sure his hearing is checked whenever you take him for his regular general physical exam.

Give Children Opportunities to Use Language

You will find almost every part of speech represented in the two-year-old's vocabulary. If they have the ability to convey their needs, thoughts, and desires in language—even if, on occasion, they resort to the sign language of infancy—they will be apt to have a more "even" disposition and will be less likely to have temper tantrums. The need for language development increases with children's growth and should keep pace with it. If they learn early to talk things over sensibly, they will have achieved something that will be valuable to them throughout their life. Language can be very useful to young children in emergencies and can save the parents needless anxiety. For instance, if your child can say his name and address, he will be able to tell an adult should he ever get lost. And what a help it is if your child can tell you about his aches and pains when he is sick.

Language development is sometimes delayed in children by anxious parents who anticipate their every need and thus deprive them of opportunities to express themselves. Language may be encouraged by framing questions in such a manner that they require an answer in words. For example, when your child is looking at a picture of a horse, if you were to ask him, "Where is the horse?" he could answer this question by simply touching the picture. If, on the other hand, you were to ask, "What is it?" he would need to use the words "horse" or "a horse" to answer your question.

Give your child opportunities to use the language he is hearing every day. Let him be a special messenger who delivers simple messages to other members of the family. Be sure to keep these first messages brief so he will have confidence in his own ability to repeat them correctly. When he is old enough to assume this responsibility, give him the opportunity to ask a store clerk for one or two items.

Be careful to give your child an audience when he tries to tell you something, and be generous in your praise whenever he expresses himself. Conversation flows freely over the dinner table, and you want your child to share in the conversations without dominating them.

Stories and Experiences Stimulate Language

Stories and firsthand experiences give children interesting things to talk about and help develop their ability to express themselves. Dramatizations of simple stories, puppet and shadow plays, and creative handiwork are excellent mediums to stimulate the development of language. For more ideas see chapter 17, "Creative Expression in Children," and chapter 20, "Dramatic Play" of this book.

My Book House plans for your child's language development long before he learns to talk. Begin by saying and singing some of these choice lullabies and rhymes to him, and you will be providing the words, phrases, and sentences that will form his own listening vocabulary. A child's ability to use and understand language later on will be influenced by the vocabulary you have exposed him to in infancy.

Language Development Varies in Children

Language development will vary in children according to their physical and mental growth. The two charts on the following pages indicate average vocabulary growth. The figures are based on the average of several hundred children. (See "Developing Your Child's Vocabulary," by Robert H. Seashore, in *In Your Hands*.

A Major Accomplishment

Think how difficult it is for an adult to learn a foreign language. Yet (and here we quote the philosopher Alfred North Whitehead) "the first intellectual task which confronts an infant is the acquirement of spoken language. What an appalling task, the correlation of meanings with sounds! It is a miracle of achievement."

Vocabulary Aids Readiness

It is generally agreed that if children were solely dependent on the vocabulary they hear at home, they would be at a loss to learn the larger number of new words they are expected to use and understand in the classroom. Stories and rhymes that have been carefully age-graded and illustrated will help give your child a choice variety of words he will begin to use as his own.

My Book House was planned to give your child the opportunity of hearing a good descriptive vocabulary used over and over again—a vocabulary that will make his speech more interesting and colorful. In the first three volumes alone, he will hear 6,800 different words used in a variety of interesting stories. By the time he is ready to enter first grade, your child will have acquired a vocabulary of about 2,500 words, and a listening vocabulary of about 6,800 words that will help give him confidence in expressing himself. A child with a good vocabulary is equipped to understand the language of the teacher, follow directions, and exchange ideas. He will be ready to learn! An enriched vocabulary will make him familiar with the sound and meaning of words and be a real help to him as he learns to read.

Research indicates that the family environment exerts the largest influence on a child's language development in the preschool years. It can promote a faster rate of language development, a better command of rules of grammar, and a larger vocabulary. Parents can do the following things to help promote language development in their preschool child:*

- Have conversations with your child often.
- Make conversation time a special time.
- Talk with your child in simple language (not to be confused with baby talk) that he will understand.
- Ask your child questions that require more than a simple yes or no answer.

---

*Derived from Bill Cunningham. *Child Development* (page 167). © 1993 by HarperCollins Publishers, Inc. A HarperPerennial Book reprinted by permission of HarperCollins Publishers, Inc.

▪ Repeat back to your child what he has said to make sure you understand him.

▪ Read stories and books together.

▪ Tell your child stories and encourage him to tell you stories.

Pictures Give Clue to Meaning of Words

The illustrations in *My Book House* play an important part in adding meaning to the words your child hears when you read rhymes and stories to him. For example, on page 85 in volume I, you will find this rhyme:

> *All the cats consulted;*
> *What was it about?*
> *How to catch a little mouse*
> *Running in and out.*

The illustration shows a group of cats that are clearly "talking things over." As children hear the word "consulted" in the rhyme, they observe the picture and begin associating the sound of the word "consulted" with the meaning conveyed in the picture. The rhyme and picture together help children form a concept of meaning about the new word they have heard. In the last line of "Tom, Tom, the Piper's Son," on page 34 of volume I, children hear, "Even pigs on their hind legs would after them prance." The picture illustrating this rhyme includes two little "prancing" pigs to help children form a more meaningful concept of the new word "prance."

Good Literature Influences Speech

Rhymes, poems, and stories are a natural source for descriptive words that we often fail to include in our conversation with young children. At the bottom of page 90 in volume I, you will find the rhyme

> *Bye-O! Bye-O!*
> *Baby's in the cradle sleeping.*
> *Tip-toe, tip-toe,*
> *Soft and low, like pussy creeping,*
> *Bye-O, Bye-O!*

The child who

READS

is the child who

LEADS

Children who hear this rhyme repeated will be exposed naturally to the beauty and charm of language found in the phrase "Soft and low, like pussy creeping."

Rhymes and stories play an important part in children's language development. Your child unconsciously patterns his language after the language in the stories you read to him. Young children use words, phrases, and sentences in their favorite stories to relate their own experiences. It is so important that the stories your child hears are well-written in short, well-knit sentences.

In volume I, on page 165, in the story, "Good Morning, Peter," children hear sentences like "Hello, Teddy Bear! That is what Peter said. Then he hugged Teddy Bear." This story is typical of the many familiar everyday experiences that are told in a very logical and direct manner.

In volume I, on pages 190 and 200, you will find stories about the rain and wind told in language simple enough for children to use as their own. In "A Story of the Wind" (volume I, page 200) children hear interesting sentences like "The dry leaves in the grass began to hop and flutter and fly around over the ground . . . . The trees all started to shiver, to shiver and shiver and shake . . . . The wind went capering around until it came bolting down . . . . They danced and skipped and jumped and tugged . . . ." The manner in which your child relates his own experiences will be as free, spontaneous, and interesting as the words in the stories you read to him.

Language Develops Personality

It is important for you to understand your child's language development and encourage its growth at each stage of his development. To help you in this and to give your child the background he needs as he grows and matures, great pains have been taken in the selection and the grading of the material in *My Book House.* Your child's vocabulary will grow along with his experiences and will be influenced by his choice of reading. Class discussion, assembly programs, club activities, hobbies, and class offices will be all the more attractive and interesting to a child who can express himself well. The high school student who has a good vocabulary will possess confidence, poise, and the assurance he needs to initiate his ideas and assume the role of leadership.

Speech is the basis of most communication of thought. It seems that we think primarily in words (other elements of thought being visual images and

the like), and the clarity and diversity of your child's thinking and speech will be affected by his word power. In *My Book House* the development of both a listening vocabulary and a speaking vocabulary logically begins with finger plays and nursery rhymes. As you read aloud to your child and his attention span gradually lengthens, it will soon become apparent that he is listening with his mind as well as with his ears. This, we know, is the beginning of concentration. It is your child's first preparation both for school and for understanding your simple directions at home.

Encourage language ability and a good vocabulary and you will open avenues that will promote happiness, understanding, and an interesting personality in your child. Moreover, you will be preparing him for success in life. Nothing contributes more to success in almost any field of endeavor than the ability to express one's thoughts and ideas clearly and well.

Typical references indicating vocabulary differences that are pointed out to children in *My Book House* selections are:

REFERENCES

BOATS

* "I Saw a Ship A-Sailing,"—Volume I, page 35
* "Row, Row! A-Fishing We'll Go!,"—Volume I, page 61
* "Little Beppo Pippo,"—Volume I, page 63
* "Here We Sail So Fast and Free,"—Volume I, page 96
* "My Boat,"—Volume I, page 163

HAT AND CAP

* "The Toads in the Lake,"—Volume I, page 68
* "When I See a Lady,"—Volume I, page 69
* "Hurry Up, Engine,"—Volume I, page 92
* "Yankee Doodle,"—Volume I, page 101
* "The Cap That Mother Made,"—Volume III, page 12

For more activities, see language and literature activities in various charts—chapter 15 in this book—and selections listed in index of *My Book House*, volume XII.

Language Ability

A General Growth Curve

Of The Development

Of Language

Ability

6TH YEAR Shows strong interest in the meanings of single words. Baby talk is discarded. Possesses an average vocabulary of 2,500 words and a listening vocabulary of 6,800 words.

5TH YEAR The ability to make puns and converse logically becomes apparent. Speech content implies abstract and rational thinking. Possesses an average vocabulary of about 2,200 words.

4TH YEAR Acting while talking brings enjoyment. Sentences are quite expressive of thoughts. Possesses an average vocabulary of about 1,500 words.

3RD YEAR Pleasure comes from listening to stories about familiar things. Can make sentences of 1, 2, or 3 words. Possesses an average vocabulary of about 900 words.

2ND YEAR Possesses an average vocabulary of about 250 words.

18 MONTHS Use of 2-word sentences begins, these give more meaning but are still vague. Word order becomes important in communicating meaning. Will eventually start using 3-word sentences. Possesses an average vocabulary of about 100 words.

10-15 MONTHS Speaking in one-word sentences begins where one word seems to communicate many things.

9-12 MONTHS Mimicking individual words begins.

3 MONTHS Babbling (putting together hard consonant sounds and vowels) begins. This often sounds like words.

2-4 MONTHS Cooing begins (single syllable vowels with occasional consonants).

1 MONTH Three types of cries: hunger, pain, and madness. They listen to sounds.

Vocabulary Development

The table below shows the typical acquisition rate of vocabulary in children. †

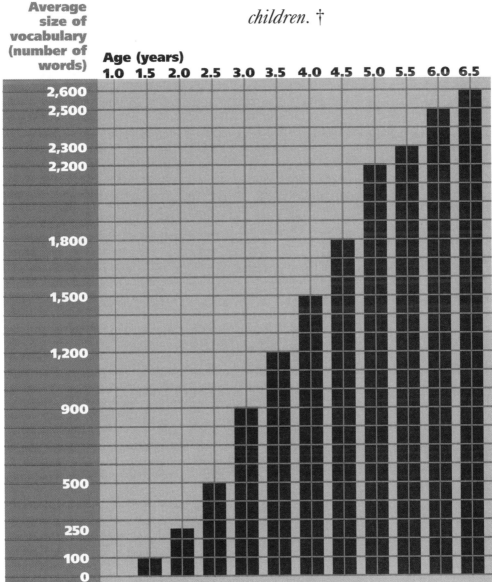

Average size of vocabulary (number of words) vs. Age (years)

† Bill Cunningham. *Child Development*, (page 166), © 1993 by HarperCollins Publishers, Inc. A HarperPerennial Book, reprinted by permission of HarperCollins Publishers, Inc.

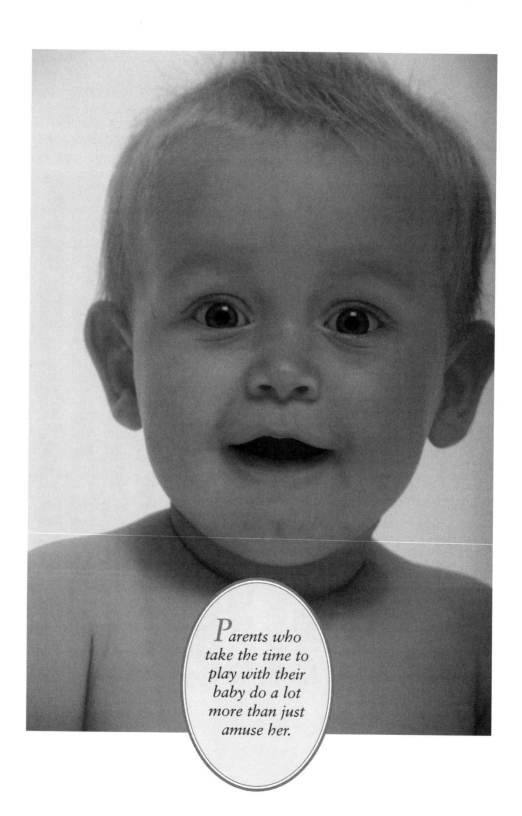

Parents who take the time to play with their baby do a lot more than just amuse her.

4

Finger Plays Do
Much More Than Amuse

Down through the ages parents have delighted in talking and playing with their babies to win their smiles, coos, and gurgles. However, few of these parents have ever stopped to realize the far-reaching influence this play will have in encouraging a happy and cooperative disposition in their babies. Parents who take the time to talk and play with their baby are doing much more than amusing her. In reality, parents are helping their child form the important habits of listening and concentrating, and they are encouraging the qualities of alertness and curiosity.

Finger plays and action rhymes like "Pat-a-Cake, Pat-a-Cake, Baker's Man" and "This Little Pig Went to Market" will help satisfy the baby's natural instinct for play and action.

Language comprehension and use in babies is closely tied to their sensory experiences of hearing, feeling, touching, seeing, tasting, and smelling. Babies use the senses to become familiar with the things around them. They learn about parents' clothes and the shape of their bottle and rattle through touching them. They learn to recognize the sound of their rattle, the song of birds, the meow of the cat, and the bark of the dog by listening. They quickly learn to distinguish the sound of the voices of the people who care for their needs. Babies use their sense of smell to help identify their baby powder, apple juice, milk, and so forth.

Finger plays and simple games where babies play an active part provide opportunities for them to gain control of their bodies and encourage certain positive dispositions. Babies must pay very close attention to parents if they want to hear, see, and do the things parents are doing as they play with them. Children learn early to detect changes in the sound of parental voices and to follow their motions. The following finger plays have been especially prepared to accompany the rhymes in *My Book House*. These finger plays will encourage your baby to enter into the activity spontaneously.

See-Saw Sacaradown
VOLUME I, PAGE 18

See-Saw, Sacaradown,
Which is the way to London town?
One foot up, the other down,
This is the way to London town.

Parents play this rhyme with the baby down in the crib, baby carriage, or couch. Lift right and left leg up and down alternately in "see-saw" motion as you say the words of the rhyme.

Pease-Porridge Hot, Pease-Porridge Cold
VOLUME I, PAGE 47

Pease-porridge hot, pease-porridge cold,
Pease-porridge in the pot, nine days old.
Some like it hot, some like it cold,
Some like it in the pot, nine days old.

For younger babies, clap hands together three times to words "Pease-porridge hot." Repeat for "Pease-porridge cold." Clap hands gently against baby's legs to "Pease-porridge in the pot, nine days old." Repeat action of first line for the third line. Repeat action of the second line for the fourth line.

Pat-a-Cake, Pat-a-Cake, Baker's Man

VOLUME I, PAGE 19

Pat-a-cake, pat-a-cake, baker's man!
Make me a cake as fast as you can;
Prick it and pat it, mark it with T,
And put it in the oven for Tommy
and me.

For younger children At first, hold baby's wrists in your hands and clap his hands together rhythmically as you say the rhyme. Later, the rhyme may be repeated facing the baby so he can see what you are doing and clap his own hands as the words are repeated. He will soon try imitating your actions. After you have played the rhyme with him a few times, he will begin to clap his own hands together on hearing the words.

Suggestion for older children Older children will enjoy a little variety in the actions for "Pat-a-cake." Here is a suggested form: Clap hands in rhythm with the first line of the rhyme. Then for the line "Prick it, and pat it" fold right hand in a fist and extend forefinger. Now, make a motion similar to one you would use if you were to prick the top of a pie, and then pat your hands together. For the remainder of the line "and mark it with T" hold the left hand straight up and rigid and place the right hand across the top of it to form the letter T. For the last line, "And put it in the oven for Tommy and me," extend both hands forward with palms up as if you were actually putting a pan of cookies in the oven. Using the right hand, point away from you to indicate Tommy and toward you to indicate yourself.

Humpty Dumpty Sat on a Wall

VOLUME I, PAGE 46

Humpty Dumpty sat on a wall,
Humpty Dumpty had a great fall.
All the king's horses and all the king's men,
Couldn't put Humpty Dumpty together again.

Hold hands together in clapping position as you say, "Humpty Dumpty sat on a wall." Drop hands to lap suddenly to "Humpty Dumpty had a great fall." Turn hands palms up and spread fingers apart to the last two lines.

This Little Pig Went to Market

VOLUME I, PAGE 19

This little pig went to market;
This little pig stayed at home;
This little pig had roast beef;
This little pig had none;
This little pig said, "Wee, wee, wee!
I can't find my way home!"

Play this with your baby by touching each toe as you tell about the five little pigs. When you come to the last little pig who cried "Wee, wee, wee," you can wiggle the baby's little toe. This can also be played using fingers instead of toes.

Hickory, Dickory, Dock
VOLUME I, PAGE 22

Hickory, dickory, dock!
The mouse ran up the clock;
The clock struck one, the mouse ran down,
Hickory, dickory, dock!

Nod head from side to side to the words,
"Hickory, dickory, dock." Raise both arms as
high as you can reach with fingers in motion
as you say the line, "The mouse ran up the
clock." Keep arms raised over head and clap
hands together for "The clock struck one."
Return arms to side with fingers in motion to
"The mouse ran down." Finish with nods of
head from right to left to the last line,
"Hickory, dickory, dock."

Jack and Jill Went Up the Hill
VOLUME I, PAGE 40

Jack and Jill went up the hill
To fetch a pail of water;
Jack fell down and broke his crown
And Jill came tumbling after.

Raise both arms over your head as
you repeat the lines, "Jack and Jill
went up the hill / To fetch a pail of
water." Drop one arm suddenly to
"Jack fell down and broke his
crown." Drop the other arm suddenly to "And Jill came tumbling after."

Giuseppi, the Cobbler
VOLUME I, PAGE 63

Giuseppi, the cobbler, makes my shoes;
He pounds them, rap, rap, rap!
He makes them small, he makes them big,
And ever he pounds, tap, tap!

Tap fists together in time with the rhyme "Giuseppi, the cobbler, makes my shoes; / He pounds them, rap, rap, rap!" Hold hands close together as you say, "He makes them small." Spread hands farther apart to "He makes them big." Tap fists together again to "And ever he pounds, tap, tap!"

Row, Row!
A-Fishing We'll Go!
VOLUME I, PAGE 61

Row, row! A-fishing we'll go!
How many fishes have you, Joe?
One for my father, one for my mother,
One for my sister, one for my brother,
And one for the little fisher boy!

Move arms back and forth in rowing motion to "Row, row! A-fishing we'll go!" Continue same movement with "How many fishes have you, Joe?" Hold left hand in folded position and with right hand unfold each finger beginning with thumb to "One for my father," and so on.

There Were Two Blackbirds
VOLUME I, PAGE 52

There were two blackbirds
Sitting on a hill,
The one named Jack,
And the other named Jill.
Fly away, Jack!
Fly away, Jill!
Come again, Jack!
Come again, Jill!

Make fists with thumbs extended to "There were two blackbirds." Bring fists together with "Sitting on a hill." Extend right fist to "The one named Jack." Extend left fist to "And the other named Jill." Open right hand and move hand outward in fluttering motion to "Fly away, Jack!" Open left hand and move hand outward in fluttering motion to "Fly away, Jill!" Bring hands back to starting position to the lines "Come again, Jack! / Come again, Jill!"

Here's the Church
VOLUME I, PAGE 83

Here's the church,
And here's the steeple:
Open the door
And see all the people!

For younger children Interlock fingers with "Here's the church." Extend forefingers to "And here's the steeple." Spread thumbs apart to "Open the door." Unfold fingers and wiggle them to "And see all the people!"

Suggestion for older children   Children lock hands, fingers down, thumbs close together to represent the church door, and forefingers up and joined for the spire. With "Open the door!" they open their hands, fingers still locked, and wiggle the fingers to represent the people.

Finger plays help develop alertness in young babies, who soon come to associate certain actions with the sounds of words and phrases they hear you repeat in rhymes and jingles. Babies form habits of speech very early, so it is important that the language your baby hears from the very beginning is rhythmical, clear, and musical. The love of good language will color your baby's impressions, and, once again, his speech will reflect the same language qualities he has heard from birth.

Additional actions, rhymes, and jingles to play with your baby are listed in the index of *My Book House*, volume XII, on page 263 under "Games and Rhythms."

*P*arents
can be seen as
sympathetic
shapers of
their child's
personality.

5

Bring Out the Best in Your Child's Personality

Babies are born with different styles of responding to their environment, or temperament. Thus, babies enter the world with individual differences in characteristics such as activity level, fussiness, soothability, shyness, or sociability.

Temperament*

While the notion of temperament has been around since ancient Greece, and parents and nursery workers have long recognized these individual differences in infants, social scientists did not begin actively researching temperament until this century. One group of researchers, led by Drs. Alexander

---

*Temperament material derived from *A to Z Guide to Your Children's Behavior.* Compiled by the Children's National Medical Center under the direction of David Mrazek and William

Thomas, Stella Chess, and Herbert Birch, followed 133 children from their birth to adulthood. Through the study, begun in the 1950s, the researchers identified the following eight temperamental qualities:

1. Regularity of biological functions, such as sleeping, eating, and bowel movements.
2. Activity level or the degree to which children like to move about or sit still.
3. Distractibility or ability to concentrate.
4. Persistence or lack thereof in accomplishing goal-oriented tasks.
5. Predominant quality of mood, e.g., cheerful and easygoing versus irritable and whiny.
6. Degree of adaptability to new stimuli ranging from quick to slow adjustment.
7. Approach to or withdrawal from new stimuli.
8. Intensity of expressed mood or emotion.

From research, it appears that the temperamental qualities that tend to persist most through an individual's life involve sociability, emotionality, and physical activity level. It should be noted that researchers disagree on which qualities or traits should be called temperamental. One thing they overwhelmingly agree upon, however, is that behavioral tendencies such as these are greatly influenced by the environment and are thus modifiable. Further, most children do not show extremes of these dispositions and fall somewhere in the middle.

Thus, parenting and the family environment play a crucial role in shaping children's personalities. Dealing with conflict, communication, and values are just some of the areas where parental behavior can have a profound affect on children. Easygoing babies can be made more difficult or hostile through neglect or abuse. And, conversely, more difficult children can be made more

Garrison with Laura Elliott (pages 294-298). © 1993 by the Children's National Medical Center. A Perigee Book, The Putnam Berkley Group.

And from H. Hill Goldsmith (Convener), Arnold H. Buss, Robert Plomin, Mary Klevjord Rothbart, Alexander Thomas and Stella Chess, Robert A. Hinde (Commentator), and Robert B. McCall (Commentator). Roundtable: What is Temperament? Four Approaches. Child Development, 58, (pages 505-529), © 1987 by the Society for Research in Child Development, Inc.

†"What Is Temperament? Four Approaches," *Child Development*, 58 (pages 505–529). © 1987 by the Society for Research in Child Development, Inc.

easygoing with patient support and guidance. Parents, then, can be seen as sympathetic shapers of their child, helping to change or strengthen inborn dispositions in ways to help their child's positive development. As the adults, it is up to the parents to adapt their personality and parenting style to fit their child's tendencies.

Knowing children are born with behavioral tendencies may be comforting to parents who have experienced frustration dealing with a child who shows extremes in some of these tendencies. It is hoped that this knowledge will help parents to be more tolerant of their child's individuality, as well as more tolerant of themselves and the inevitable frustrations and difficulties of being a parent.

The feeling of being loved, of being secure, which you communicate to your child from the time she is born, is the most essential factor in her personality development. And the love and affection she feels for you, as well as her desire for your approval, play a large role in motivating her to become socialized, to learn to suffer disappointment, and to make the numerous adjustments in life she will need to.

While you are encouraging positive tendencies, others may need to be redirected. Suppose your child expresses an unwillingness to go to bed. She is not being naughty intentionally; she is simply not ready for what is expected of her. To meet this situation, read her one or two bedtime rhymes or poems. (See list in index of *My Book House* under heading Child's Daily Activities, volume XII, page 289.) Repeat the lines quietly and softly, and it will help her become ready for sleep. Similarly, a little sleepy-head may be aroused by hearing the rhyme "Wake Up, Jacob" repeated in a happy tone of voice.

Parents Decide Atmosphere of the Home

Parents decide the home atmosphere through their daily mode of living. It is the parents' responsibility to set the stage for good habit formation and dispositions in their child. The first duty of parents should be to take inventory of their own emotional reactions to see that the child is exposed to positive dispositions in the home. The urge to be cheerful, thoughtful, and friendly is caught rather than taught. Children quickly accept cheerfulness, good nature, love, friendliness, or moodiness as the order of the day, and it is only natural that the attitudes children are exposed to most frequently will become more or less automatic with them. Love and understanding, firmness tempered with justice, and patience with their shortcomings will give your child a feeling of security and encourage the development of the qualities you want her to possess and reflect. Kindness and helpfulness in the home will help bring out courtesy and friendliness in your child's nature. The tone of your voice, your mannerisms, the touch of your hands as you bathe and dress her give her clues to your frame of mind and challenge her to match your attitude and disposition.

Do not expect perfection in your child's behavior and be careful not to demand more of her than she is capable of giving. The growth of worthwhile habits, character qualities, and an attractive personality is a gradual one and cannot be hurried. Temper tantrums and "No, I won'ts" frequently come from exposing children to situations they are unable to cope with successfully. They reveal their feeling of frustration and indicate their lack of confidence to meet the situation at hand. Emotions are among the most powerful influences in life, and the young child, as well as the adult, gains the necessary poise and ability to guide and control them through experience, perseverance, and desire.

Importance of Habit Formation

The habits young children form soon become automatic and help ease the strain of the day's routine. As soon as they have formed habits that help them eat, dress, put toys away, etc., they will be relieved of some emotional strain and find more joy in their activities. By age five children should possess a set of habits that will leave them free to initiate ideas, think things through for themselves, concentrate, and act independently. Kindergarten and first grade programs are planned around children who are ready to act and think independently. The habits your child forms during her early years will greatly affect her readiness for learning and her ability to make adjustments with friends and playmates.

Accept your child's offers to help and encourage her independence at every stage where she is capable of assuming responsibility for her own actions. Give her plenty of time to try putting her toys away, buttoning and unbuttoning her clothes, and attempting to feed herself. Hurrying her in this initial stage of independence will only confuse her and rob her of the thrill that comes with accomplishment. It is important that she be cooperative when she is getting washed and dressed, that she go to bed willingly, and that she be cheerful and friendly in her contacts with people. Young children instinctively imitate what they see and hear, and rhymes and stories that present friendliness, willing obedience, truthfulness and self-control in an attractive manner will suggest many desirable qualities that children will accept as their own.

Stories Influence Character Development

A variety of rhymes and stories that will help bring out positive qualities in your child are listed in the index, volume XII, under Child's Daily Activities on page 289. The finger plays beginning on page 30 of this book will encourage a happy, cheerful disposition in your baby; while stories similar to "Good Morning, Peter" (volume I, page 165) will delight and challenge the youngster who is learning to dress herself. Do not attempt to moralize the stories you read to her. Let the stories tell their own message in the delightful story language that your child understands and enjoys. *My Book House* lists age-graded selections under such qualities as Courage, Honesty, and Perseverance. For example, "The Little Engine That Could" (volume II, page 200) is listed under Perseverance. Every child will enjoy hearing about the plucky little engine that worked so hard to pull the trainload of toys over a high mountain so the children who lived on the other side could have them in time for Christmas. The engine kept saying, "I think I can! I think I can!" The mountainside was steep and the load was heavy, but the little engine kept trying and saying, "I think I can!" until it finished what it had started out to do. It then ran gaily down the other side of the mountain saying, "I thought I could! I thought I could!" Perhaps you will find your child imitating the Little Engine with this "I think I can! I thought I could!" attitude when she is putting her toys away or doing some other chore around the house. This "I think I can!" attitude will serve her well in so many situations throughout life.

Good or bad habits are the result of frequent repetition. In using stories to their full advantage it is necessary to make reading a habit and set aside a regular reading time each day as a story hour. Bedtime is the ideal story time because then the little one is generally content to sit or lie quietly and listen. It is then, too, that they are most likely to beg "Daddy, Mommy, read me a story." Sharing a regular reading time, among other benefits, helps bring about a closer bond of understanding between parent and child.

Stories present life situations to children in a personal way and act as an incentive for them to develop the same tolerance, loyalty, and courage manifested in their story friends. They are an important part of their mental diet and a vital influence in helping children form their own code for living. By carefully choosing from the story index, you often will touch upon situations which have or may come up in your child's day. Solutions the story characters find for their problems may well help your child smooth over an unpleasant situation at home or school. Make use of a story background and you will find yourself looking at your child's behavior more objectively and impersonally. And you will be "building bridges" into your child's world.

Encourage Your Child to Make Decisions

It is often easier for parents to give a command than it is for them to use the ingenuity that is required for intelligent control of a behavior situation. Children who are taught only through command are very often helpless in a real-life situation. You want them to feel able to make simple decisions for themselves and to act with confidence when they are in school or at play. If you continually teach them to wait for your decision before they act, they will lose opportunities to think for themselves. The manner in which they are able to meet their everyday problems now will help them to make decisions in more complex problems later on. Be patient and ready to praise your child's sincere efforts to adjust to the situations she must meet. It is only in this way that she will acquire the self-assurance she needs to adjust to situations later in life.

Parents sometimes forget that a child's eye view of the world is that of a world of legs—a world of giants. Even the walls of the room an infant is creeping in can reach to an interminable height. In Denmark, a country noted for its fine educational system, a room has been built for parents out of proportion to their size to enable them to perceive what an "outsized" world babies live in. In this room the doorknobs are almost out of reach and a spoon is as large as a ladle. Exploring this room, parents become aware of the adjustments young children must make to their physical world. Thus they have the perspective they need in order to help their child make, with ease and confidence, the adjustments that are necessary to their growth. Children that feel at home with people possess one of the most valuable assets for assuring their continued success and happiness. A sympathetic understanding of their problems will do much to bring this about.

My Book House is filled with characters from the literature of the world who will influence your child's personality and make her more tolerant and considerate of the opinions and customs of others. Stories help enrich children's experiences and give them the benefit of hearing others make wise decisions. They will readily accept the desirable behavior patterns and decisions of the storybook and real friends they admire. Just imagine the impression "The Tale of Peter Rabbit" (volume II, page 112) would have on young children who are reluctant to obey parental requests on matters important to their safety and welfare. It is quite within children's comprehension to decide that Peter was most foolish to disobey his mother's advice, "don't go into Mr. McGregor's garden."

REFERENCES

A few examples of the character building selections in *My Book House* are listed below. For a complete list, see the Character Building Index of *My Book House*, volume XII, page 288.

COURAGE

Shingebess, the brave, cheery, little brown duck, (volume II, page 96) will help your child overcome fear and timidity, and encourage sticking to the task at hand.

COOPERATION

Li'l' Hannibal (volume II, page 116) was unwilling to do his share so he decided to run away and live with the birds and animals. But no one could stop and play for there was too much work to be done! When Li'l' Hannibal learned he couldn't have any supper because he hadn't helped, he decided for himself that he had better go home and be willing to do his share. Your child will learn from this story to cooperate and see a thing through to its finish.

PERSEVERANCE

"The Little Engine That Could" (volume II, page 200) will help your young child understand the importance of an attitude of determination. Boys and girls will be thrilled to hear how the Little Engine, against great odds, achieved a goal which seemed impossible. This story will set a positive example for a child who is inclined toward discouragement, or one who is tempted to give up too easily.

Older readers will find in volume XII, many examples of persons whose achievements were realized in spite of great obstacles and handicaps.

STUBBORNNESS

This story may help soften indications of stubbornness. The antics of the "Big, Contrary Coo" in the story "The Wee, Wee Mannie and the Big, Big Coo" (volume III, page 99), will help your child see how foolish it is to be stubborn. She will decide for herself that she does not want to be like the ridiculous old cow who simply "would not stand still."

See Social Behavior and Adjustment Qualities in various charts in chapter 15 of this book.

For selections to encourage desirable habits, attitudes, character and disposition qualities see Character Building Index of *My Book House*, volume XII, page 288.

Your child's problems

like her hands

may look SMALL *in comparison to yours, but for her they are* BIG *enough.*

*P*atiently
answering your
child's many
questions can
bring him back
to you again
and again.

6

Can You Answer
Your Child's Questions?

QUESTIONING AND CURIOSITY are part of growth. Babies find the world around them a continual challenge and they are constantly seeking information. Your child's questions reflect his thinking and attempts at reasoning, and they give him the opportunity to practice language. In addition, his thinking processes are stimulated by talking with others. Be patient and calm during this often trying developmental period, and before long you will acquire the art of answering his questions in a manner that will prove helpful to both of you.

Children who question are thinking and alert, and one can see their active minds growing. Your own ability to answer your child's questions will establish confidence in him and bring him back again and again to seek your advice. If you continually show irritation and annoyance when he questions you, he may lose his desire to investigate and reason and turn to others for answers.

Stages in Questioning

Children's questions can confuse parents who must stop to think how to put the answer into language simple enough for them to understand. If you are familiar with the various stages of questioning in young children, you will be more successful in your approach. Some questions require only one-word answers, while others must be dealt with in more detail. For the most part, parents err on the side of boring young children with detailed answers beyond their comprehension. Give them an answer to satisfy their present needs and they will come back later when they need further information.

Questions of Two- and Three-Year-Olds

Two- to three-year-olds often ask questions to hear themselves talk. They love to use their newly acquired language and for the most part know the answers to the questions they ask. They may be satisfied sometimes to have you ask them the same question they asked you. This gives them an opportunity to tell you the answer and, above all, they crave your attention and an occasion to talk. "Where's the book," "See the cow?" and "Where's Stuart?" are typical questions of this age.

Questions of Four- and Five-Year-Olds

Questioning is at its peak in four-year-olds. Their questions sometimes reflect their love of talking and need for your attention more than a hunger for new information. Indeed, they ask many why and how questions but are not always interested in explanations. Children's questions at this age are an opportunity for them to use language and formulate relationships in their own mind. They gain better control of language through asking questions, and they begin adding clauses, adjectives, and adverbs to their vocabulary. "I *was* a good boy, wasn't I?" or "I *was* the best runner, wasn't I?" are typical questions of the four-year-old. Very often there is no answer to the four-year-old's questions, and a story that implies an answer will often satisfy them best. The traffic light at the corner may attract their attention and their questions about them are often their way of thinking out loud about this new experience. "The Big Street in the Big City" (volume I, page 170), "Policeman

Joe" (volume I, page 173), and "Biting Marion" (volume I, page 174) are stories telling of experiences similar to their own. Choose one of these stories to answer their questions, and you will not only satisfy their curiosity at the moment, but you will expose them to additional details that they will want to observe for themselves.

Children of four or five who question you about the wind will be more interested in a story or verse that tells about its usefulness than in a scientific explanation.

> *Blow, wind, blow, and go, mill, go!*
> *That the miller may grind his corn;*
> *That the baker may take it,*
> *And into rolls make it,*
> *And send us some hot in the morn.*

(FROM "BLOW, WIND, BLOW," *MY BOOK HOUSE* VOLUME I, PAGE 31).

This rhyme not only gives children a satisfying answer, but it also provides information they can understand and enjoy.

Five-year-old children will often be more direct in their questions; they are seeking definite information. By five, they no longer ask questions merely for attention and practice in speaking. They will be more interested in knowing how a traffic light works and what makes the light turn from green to red. Their questions may be easier to deal with than the four-year-old's because they have more meaning and reason for being asked and because they have accumulated a background of experiences that help them understand the things you refer to in your answers. They will want an answer in terms of use and are able to understand answers with details. They are also capable of questioning the meaning of a particular word.

When your child asks a question that puzzles you, do not hesitate to say, "Let's look it up and see what the book says." Never postpone or sidestep giving an answer to any legitimate question, no matter how unimportant it may seem to you. If parents do not answer children's information-seeking questions, children will soon stop asking them, and it may stunt their interest in people and things around them. It is partly through asking questions that children learn. But because their interest span is short, keep your answers simple and on the level of their understanding. And do not give too much by the way of explanation. Never laugh at your child's ignorance; treat his questions with respect and do all that you can to encourage his growing desire for knowledge.

In his fine article "Help Your Child Find the Answers" in *Your Child's World*, Everett E. Sentman says, "Curiosity is a divine gift. It is the mental hunger which leads the child to adapt himself to life on this planet. If you stimulate (you cannot satisfy) the young child's natural curiosity, you help to develop mental attitudes that will open doors of discovery for him all his life."

A Good Encyclopedia, Dictionary, and Atlas Are Invaluable

Good reference books are important not only for the facts they contain but, of equal importance, for the encouragement they can give to the "look-it-up" habit. Accurate illustrations and understandable definitions and explanations, combined with the example of parents using these resources, help establish the important "I wonder" to "I know" to "I know how to know" sequence of the inquiring mind.

Stories and Pictures Help Answer Your Child's Questions

Books and accurate pictures not only help to answer a child's questions but enable him to find for himself many of the answers he is seeking. Throughout all the grades, his curiosity will spur him on to read and investigate in order to find the information he needs. The selections and pictures in *My Book House* will do much to keep you informed of your child's interests and will enable you to share these interests with him as he progresses.

Importance of Biographies

Volume XII of *My Book House* is a treasury of biographies. Written in appealing story form, many of the biographies bring to life admirable persons from the world of literature. They are told briefly, simply, and dramatically to satisfy children's curiosity about some of the authors and poets who contributed to *My Book House*. Other sketches in volume XII relate the inspiring events of outstanding persons across numerous fields, such as science, the arts, and sports.

Besides the biographical sketches in volume XII, in other volumes *My Book House* contains inspiring and exciting stories about such famous people as George Washington, Abraham Lincoln, David Farragut, Daniel Boone, and Buffalo Bill Cody. The selections are listed under Biographical Sketches in the Special Subjects index of volume XII. Stories that combine the elements of biography and fiction, such as "The Boy Hero of Harlem," "The Knights of the Silver Shield," "The Story of Big Paul Bunyan," "Dick Whittington and His Cat," and "The Exile of Rama" make fascinating reading for grade school children and give them a background of knowledge that will add color and zest to their study of history, geography, and social science. They may also stimulate their interest in further research and in reading fiction.

It is recommended that you read the preface of volume XII of *My Book House* for a further explanation of the value of biographies in the development of sound character traits in your child and in providing a background for their growing interest in the world's best literature.

References

SUGGESTIONS FOR THE YOUNG CHILD

See selections listed in index of *My Book House*, volume XII, under:

(See also in this book, "Holidays Begin at Home," chapter 19; "Let Your Child Discover the Joy of Music," chapter 21; "Expose Your Child to Nature Experiences," chapter 10; and "Dramatic Play," chapter 20, which has suggestions for encouraging imitation and dramatic play in your child.)

SUGGESTIONS FOR THE OLDER CHILD

See selections listed in index of *My Book House*, volume XII, under:

So little time. . .

In preschool years you have

your child twenty-four hours a day. . .

the days drag by

but the years

fly by

It's agreed that children who are ready to learn are also eager to learn.

7

Encourage Your Child's Natural Readiness for Learning

THE EXPERIENCES parents provide for their child will largely determine her ability to adjust to the world. Her home environment and early experiences help set the stage for her mental maturity and readiness for learning. The baby of six months is not physically ready to walk and talk, but she is ready to sit up by herself and crow and squeal with delight. The one-year-old has comparatively few words in his vocabulary, while the two-year-old is ready to use three or even four words in phrases and sentences.

Children who are ready to learn are eager to learn. During their preschool days they must learn many things in order to be happy and comfortable with their friends and playmates. Social adjustment and personal responsibility truly begin in infancy. Wise parents will not wait to discover readiness for learning in the child, they will plan a rich background of experiences that will add meaning to children's interpretations of the things around them. Such a background will include a wealth of firsthand and story experiences to encourage language ability, social adjustment, personal responsibility, and a chance to mature fully at each age level. In addition it is good to provide play materials and equipment that give children opportunities to investigate and create.

School Programs Planned Around Readiness of Child

Programs are planned to suit the readiness of children enrolled. By kindergarten age, children should have formed the habit of listening so that they will be ready to listen to learn. The kindergarten program is planned for children who are familiar with creative materials like clay, paint, crayons, etc. It is planned around children with a background of rhymes, poems, stories, and experiences to help them understand the language of the schoolroom. By kindergarten age, children should be ready to help themselves and act independently. The child who has formed good work habits will be cooperative and courteous in his relationship with other children and *ready* to make his adjustments to new situations with ease.

Children who are ready to learn are more likely to experience success rather than discouragement or failure. Each new experience children encounter will be influenced by the preparation they have had to understand or interpret it. If the parent attempts to force learning situations on children that are beyond their mental maturity and comprehension, they may create a feeling of inferiority and discouragement that will handicap children for further learning. Let your child's mental maturity set his standards for learning, and he will be more successful in his first school contacts.

My Book House will encourage your child's natural readiness for learning at each phase of his development. The selections are woven around children's interests and are at their level of understanding. Using *My Book House Plan* in your home will keep you in touch with your child's needs and desires and provide an enriched story and experience background to nurture his mental maturity and readiness to learn. It will enable you to meet your child on his own level of understanding and give him experiences to guide him to happiness and success in his social, mental, and emotional adjustments.

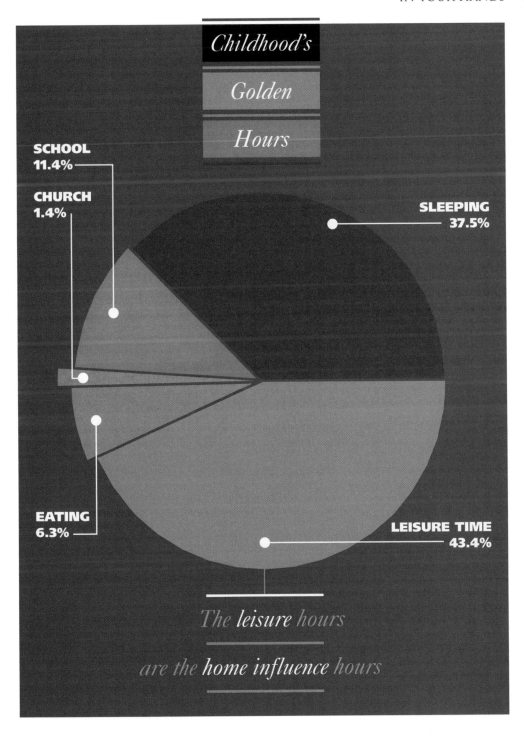

Childhood's

Golden

Hours

SCHOOL
11.4%

CHURCH
1.4%

SLEEPING
37.5%

EATING
6.3%

LEISURE TIME
43.4%

The leisure hours

are the home influence hours

Children will more likely share thoughts and emotions with parents who play with them.

8

Can You Enter Into the Spirit of Play With Your Child?

IN CHILDHOOD, play is spontaneously entered into in a joyous and free-spirited manner.* Children seem to need to play for the sake of playing. Through play children attempt new things and master them; they investigate and explore their environment; they stimulate their senses; and they exercise their growing bodies through movement. In addition to the above, play serves many more functions, one of the most important, perhaps, being that it is just plain fun.

Infants play by mimicking their adult caregivers, which helps them to form bonds with the adults. Through their kicking, cooing, smiling, and other activities, the babies are mastering basic motor skills, and through such

---

*Play material derived from *A to Z Guide to Your Children's Behavior*. Compiled by the Children's National Medical Center under the direction of David Mrazek and William Garrison with Laura Elliott (pages 201-206). © 1993 by the Children's National Medical Center. A Perigee Book, The Putnam Berkley Group.

activities as lifting and dropping their bottle, they are learning about cause and effect, that is, that when they loosen their grip on objects, they fall. Babies learn other important lessons through play. For example, through the game peekaboo, they seem to learn that things continue to exist even when they can no longer see them.

Throughout childhood many aspects of the world are learned about through play. Children learn about how objects relate to each other, for instance, if they fit together or if they work together. They learn about the size, shape, texture, and weight of objects. They learn about cause and effect and the consequences of their own and others, behaviors. Through play children also learn how to solve particular problems whether physical or social. Moreover, they learn general rules about how to approach certain types of problems. Play also serves as a forum in which children learn about the give and take of social interaction and learn important social skills, such as how to make friends, how to share, and how to express anger.

Imaginary or fantasy play can help children work out unpleasant emotions like anger, anxiety, or helplessness. It enables children to practice or rehearse their behavior in situations that they may find troubling, overwhelming, or incomprehensible. In play-acting, the situations may become more familiar and less daunting through sheer repetition. Fantasy play can also allow children to "master" the situation and thus make it less scary and more comprehensible. Finally, imaginary play helps develop children's imagination and creativity, qualities that are enjoyable in and of themselves that also aid the development of problem solving and abstract thinking.

Playing with your children strengthens your communication and overall relationship with them. They are more likely to discuss their thoughts and emotions with parents, or any adult, who plays with them. Indeed, play may allow a parent to better understand some of their child's private thoughts, feelings, and fantasies. Play is vital to children's growth and well-being, and a natural outlet for their ideas and emotions.

Helping Children's Play

Provide shelves and chests for toys and play materials, and you will greatly simplify the task of putting things away. Children get definite and meaningful training in responsibility when they have a place to house and care for their own toys and belongings.

"Pick-Up" Time

Be sure that your attitude at "pick-up" time is a cheerful and helpful one, and you will be more successful in getting your child to cooperate in putting her toys away. Very often children become so engrossed in their play that they are reluctant to obey when told to stop. Nursery and kindergarten teachers have found that children accept a signal telling them to put their playthings away more willingly than they will a hurried command like, "Put your toys away!" Clapping, snapping, ringing a bell, honking a horn, or ringing an alarm clock can be used to signal that it is time for her to begin ending play. Explain that the first signal is telling her to "Get ready now," while the second signal will mean "Come to Mom or Dad." The time allowed between two signals will depend largely upon the length of time she needs to do a good job of putting away toys and materials she's been using. A five-minute period is usually sufficient for "cleaning up." However, it may be necessary to allow more time if there has been block building or other activities where there are a lot of materials to be put away.

Toddlers find a real joy and satisfaction in doing things for themselves. Early in her training you can help her form the habit of putting her toys away. You will want her to feel she is doing her part of the job, and some simple statement like "You put your blocks on the shelf while I put your zebra in the cupboard" will help give her a feeling of satisfaction in cooperating. Give some thought to her first play experiences, and you are certain to encourage a more cooperative and helpful attitude. "Pick-up" time should serve a definite purpose in training your child in the formation of good work habits.

Choose Toys With Care

Toys and play materials that are wisely chosen will serve many purposes. Do not overlook the value of toys made from odds and ends of materials found around the house, as they are often more acceptable to children than the more elaborate and expensive ones you buy at the store.

Psychologists suggest keeping the following in mind when choosing toys for your child:

- Is it suitable for the child's age? (If it is too simple, it will not appeal to her; if it is too difficult, she will be discouraged by her inability to use it.)
- Is it practical and suitable for use in your home or yard?
- Is it sturdy enough for your child to use, yet appealing in color and design?
- Is it safe and sanitary?
- Will it promote and suggest activity that will develop her imagination and satisfy her desire to experiment and explore?

Play Reflects a Child's Maturity

The toys children enjoy at different age levels will vary with their mental maturity and physical development. Children work out their ideas in their play, so as their ideas and knowledge grow, the character of their play will change. A background of stories and experiences will help give your child a better knowledge of life, develop her imagination and thinking, and give her ideas to use in her play experiences.

Importance of a Sense of Humor

In order to see life in proper perspective, children must develop a sense of humor at a very early age. They may have been born with a tendency toward a sense of humor, but this needs a chance to grow, as any other tendency does. It may even need to be cultivated. Parents sometimes put too much stress on the seriousness of life.

The right kind of reading experience can contribute greatly to an unfolding appreciation of real humor, especially if it is shared with someone else. Throughout *My Book House* there are humorous rhymes, stories, and poems that parents and children can enjoy together. And the illustrations are always in the mood of the story or poem. Careful age-grading of the material assures parents that their child will have the right thing at the right time. Beginning with the simple humor of folk rhymes and folk tales, humor of a more subtle kind is gradually introduced. For instance, in volume III, you will find A. A. Milne's classic poem, "King Hilary and the Beggarman," which combines literary excellence with wholesome fun. In volume XII of *My Book House*, pages 265 and 266, there are eighty-four listings in the Special Subjects Index, under the heading Humorous Rhymes and Stories. By consulting this list you will be able to select a story or poem that will fit the occasion.

It has been said that if parents would laugh more, we would need fewer psychiatrists. Nothing puts parents so quickly on an understanding level with their child as laughing with her. Try not to laugh at your child until she has reached a point of maturity she is ready to laugh at herself, with you. Shared laughter often brings relief from tensions and it lessens the chance of friction between parent and child in matters of discipline. But most of all, it heightens the joy of everyday living.

Play Develops Character and Personality

Many of the lasting and basic qualities of character and personality begin to take form in children during play contacts. Some of these include the following:

Cheerfulness	Generosity	Self-confidence
Cooperation	Helpfulness	Self-control
Courage	Honesty	Sense of humor
Courtesy	Justice	Tolerance
Fair play	Leadership	Willingness
Forgiveness	Perseverance	
Friendship	Playfulness	

The development of these qualities strengthens your child's personality and makes her a more desirable member of society. In the index (volume XII, pages 289 through 298) you will find stories listed alphabetically under these same character and personality qualities. By carefully choosing stories from the index, you will be using material to encourage these qualities.

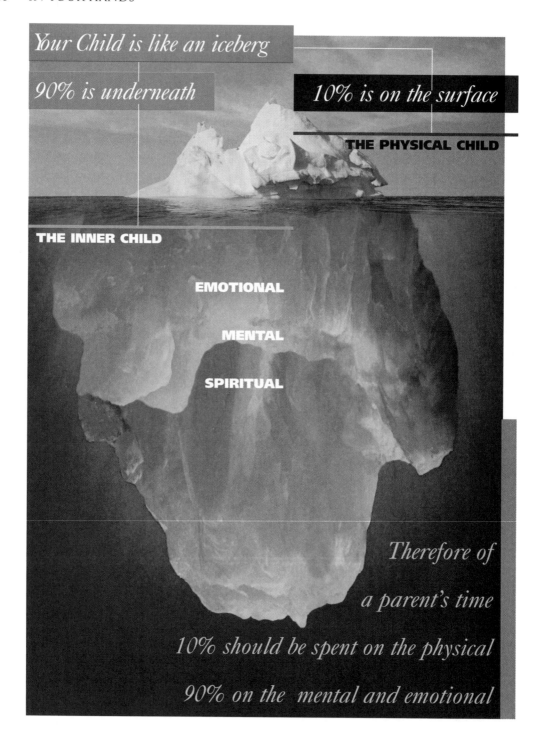

Your Child is like an iceberg

90% is underneath

10% is on the surface

THE PHYSICAL CHILD

THE INNER CHILD

EMOTIONAL

MENTAL

SPIRITUAL

Therefore of

a parent's time

10% should be spent on the physical

90% on the mental and emotional

Equip your child now for happy successful living

with these

qualities you

want for

your child

HAPPY **SOCIAL ADJUSTMENT**

GOOD **DISPOSITION HABITS**

STABLE **EMOTIONAL HABITS**

SOUND **HABIT FORMATION**

STRONG **CHARACTER BUILDING**

ROUNDED **PERSONALITY DEVELOPMENT**

Guidance can prevent

much of the emotional upset and unhappiness

children may suffer from failure.

A friendly attitude toward playmates will help your child make satisfying social adjustments.

9

Help Your Child Be Cooperative and Friendly in Early Play Contacts

Parents can do a great deal to set the stage at home for friendly play contact if they are familiar with the social behavior expected of their child from infancy through preschool.

Up until the age of fifteen or eighteen months, the baby will amuse himself for hours in his playpen, walking from one side to the other—stopping again and again to pick up, throw away, or examine the toys within his reach. He enjoys lifting objects in and out of a box, basket, or pan. His attention span is brief and so he shifts rapidly from one activity to another. He imitates things he sees other members of the family doing, and he is content to be an onlooker to the play of older children.

Generally, by the time your baby is two, he is ready to make his first play contacts with other children. While two-year-olds enjoy being in the room with other children, they are frequently at a loss to know how to play with them cooperatively. They know little of the social give-and-take necessary to group play and they rarely ask for help, so it is important for the adult to be ready to give help when it is needed.

Two-year-olds, when playing with each other, often engage in the same activities, side-by-side, and virtually ignore each other. Psychologists refer to this as "parallel play." In addition, at this age the urge to imitate is strong, and they will often want to play with the same toy their playmate is using. It is a good idea for parents to plan for the visit of a playmate in order to prevent unnecessary squabbling and tears. Put most of your child's toys out of sight for these occasions, and leave out only one or two duplicate toys that will permit the youngsters to carry on parallel play at the same time. In this way both children will be satisfied. If you realize that sharing is still beyond the child's comprehension at two, you will be able to prevent needless fussing. A wagon or ball may be left in the playroom to encourage any efforts at cooperative play. The two-year-old is very much an individual and is primarily interested in handling his play materials and in imitating the play of others.

By the time your child is three years old, he will be more mature and ready to take turns and share. His imagination and sense of dramatization will begin to enter into his play. At this age, fantasy and make-believe play large roles, and children may sometimes not be able to distinguish fact from fantasy. This is perfectly healthy and may allow children to work out difficult situations. At this age, they also become more interested in and capable of truly interactive play with other children. They will begin to use blocks to build bridges, houses, or garages and to dramatize these activities with their toys.

At four children will want to use their play material more constructively to represent the activities they have seen and enjoyed. Indeed, their ideas will often exceed their own ability to carry them out in detail.

By the time children are five, they will want to finish the things they have begun, and their interest in one activity alone may carry on for several days.

A friendly attitude toward playmates will be a real asset in helping your child make satisfying social adjustments. Playing with other children can teach him basic rules for polite social interaction. For instance, when first beginning to play with other children, he may tend to be bossy. This will usually be relatively painlessly tempered by the negative reactions of his playmates.

The rhymes, stories, and pictures in *My Book House* will suggest many activities your child may want to carry out in his play. Your child may enjoy the following selections:

* "Teddy Bear, Teddy Bear" (*My Book House*, volume I, page 91) suggests activities children may like to imitate.
* "Building with Blocks" (*My Book House*, volume I, page 64) suggests buildings children will want to try to make with their own blocks.
* "Policeman Joe" (*My Book House,* volume I, page 173), "Biting Marion" (*My Book House*, volume I, page 174), "The Big Engine" (*My Book House*, volume I, page 179), "Mister Postman" (*My Book House*, volume I, page 182) give them many ideas to carry out with their own toy trains, autos, and trucks.
* "The Snow Man" (*My Book House*, volume I, page 192) and "Snow" (*My Book House*, volume II, page 208) suggest snow activities.
* "Paper Boats" (*My Book House*, volume II, page 139) suggests making paper boats and sailing them in a tub or pond.
* "The Zoo in the Park" (*My Book House*, volume I, page 186), "The Orchestra" (*My Book House*, volume I, page 187), "The Big Umbrella and the Little Rubbers" (*My Book House*, volume I, page 190), "The Teddy Bears' Picnic" (*My Book House*, volume II, page 57), "The Circus Parade" (*My Book House*, volume III, page 46), and "A Happy Day In the City" (*My Book House*, volume III, page 181) all suggest rhythms and dramatic play that appeal to children.

Chapters 17, 18, and 20 of this book give additional aids and suggestions for creative activities that your child will want to carry out in his play.

Your child's attitude toward nature will depend largely upon your own attitude and interest in nature.

10

Expose Your Child to Nature Experiences

Parents frequently lose sight of the many opportunities they have to introduce their child to the simple wonders in nature. All too often parents are convinced that one must be a naturalist or live in the great outdoors to point out simple happenings a child will enjoy. In reality, whether we live in the crowded city or the quiet of the country, we can observe the sun, moon, stars, wind, rain, or snow, and seasonal changes. Children are curious to know more about the things they see all around them.

A walk in almost any community will give your child a chance to see trees budding in the spring or getting ready for winter. She can experience, first-hand, the change in the sun, wind, and rain as the seasons progress. Plan your walk so there is plenty of time for her to investigate the things you may want to point out, and be careful not to try to crowd too many incidents into one trip.

A child will more fully appreciate the shade from the trees if she has been allowed to stand in it on a hot day and enjoy the cool refreshment it offers. Do not be disturbed or try to hurry her if she wants to stop to pick up the fuzzy caterpillar or earthworm she has discovered for herself. It is only through these intimate contacts with nature that she will come to understand and appreciate its many mysteries. Before long she will be making many wonderful discoveries of her own and want to share them with you.

Your child's attitudes toward nature and the great outdoors, her love and appreciation of bird, animal, and plant life, will depend largely upon your own everyday attitude and interest in these same things. Nature offers parents and children many mutual experiences to further the growth of a fine relationship.

Children who are familiar with the things in nature found in their own home environment will be more alert and appreciative of beauty in the world at large. At an early age they learn to know the feel of soil and sand as they mix and pat mud pies. They can learn about the strength of wind from sailing their own boat on a pond.

Nature Rhymes and Stories Help Children Understand Natural Phenomena

Such rhymes and stories can add to child's confidence and security. Poems and stories that tell about the friendly, useful work of the rain will help allay any fears of storms, lightning, and thunder. The rain that is keeping her from outdoor play will not seem so hostile if she has heard the following friendly verses:

> *I like the rain! I like the rain!*
> *It makes the world so clean!*
> *The thirsty flowers, they drink it up—*
> *I've watched them and I've seen!*

(The above verse is from "Thunder and Lightning" in *My Book House*, volume I, page 195.)

or

> *The rain is raining all around,*
> *It falls on field and tree,*
> *It rains on the umbrellas here,*
> *And on the ships at sea.*

(The above verse is from "Rain" in *My Book House*, volume I, page 191.)

Children will discover the rhythm of the rain as it patters on their roof and windowpane. They will find mystery in the wind that is howling through the trees if they are familiar with verses such as:

Who has seen the wind?
Neither you nor I;
But when the trees bow down their heads,
The wind is passing by.

(The above verse is from "Who Has Seen the Wind" in *My Book House*, volume I, page 201.)
   or

"Come, little leaves," said the wind one day,
"Come over the meadows with me and play;
Put on your dresses of red and gold,
For summer is gone and the days grow cold."

(The above verse is from "Come, Little Leaves" in *My Book House*, volume II, page 70.)

Parents often take for granted that their child will discover all the interesting things in nature for herself, and as a result she may be deprived of fascinating experiences. Rhymes, stories, and pictures about the moon, sun, stars, birds, and animals will help awaken her interest in the familiar things around her and give them more appeal.

A Magnifying Glass Adds Interest to Nature Experiences

It encourages your child to examine the things she sees more closely. Let her save the cocoon she sees on her walk, and she is certain to be curious about the caterpillar that spun it and the beautiful butterfly that will emerge from it. Milkweed pods, nuts, stones, shells, or fallen leaves may be the beginning of a nature collection that will bring your child a great deal of pleasure. An aquarium where she can study the habits and characteristics of fish, snails, turtles, and tadpoles will delight her. Planting and caring for her own little garden, providing food for birds and pets, and arranging flowers for the table are just a few of the many other experiences that she will enjoy.

Answer your child's questions in language simple enough for her to understand, and save the more scientific explanations until she is ready to absorb them. As your child's nature experiences broaden, she will feel the need for more detailed knowledge and seek authentic references to satisfy her curiosity. During this period she may put forth tremendous effort to read scientific books on the subject most appealing to her. A children who is able to find interesting things in nature will never be at a loss for a hobby to follow in their leisure time. Experiences with nature are sure to add color and beauty to your child's speech and thought, as well as influence her desire to create.

REFERENCES

See Nature selections listed in index of *My Book House*, volume XII, under:

Animals, page 270
Birds, page 274
Farm and Country, page 262

Flowers, page 277
Seasons, page 280

See Nature Experiences and Social Science in various charts in chapter 15 of this book.

What schools expect of your child

on that first day

EXPRESSIVENESS IN WORDS AND ACTION

EXPERIENCE IN NUMBERS CONCEPTS

15 MINUTE SPAN OF CONCENTRATION

UP TO A 6,800 WORD VOCABULARY

LIVING AND LEARNING EXPERIENCE

*N*umber readiness, like reading readiness, is acquired through experience.

11

Building
Number Experiences

Nᴜᴍʙᴇʀ ʀᴇᴀᴅɪɴᴇss is acquired, like readiness for reading, through experience. The manner in which children meet number experiences in the home, before they go to school, may influence their understanding and liking for mathematics later on.

By the time children are ready to enter first grade, they are expected to know how to count to ten, and to understand the meaning of terms like big and little, long and short, full and empty, more than and less than, as well as other similar descriptive phrases. They are expected to speak of groups of two or three objects, as in two cows or three birds, without having to stop to count them individually. In other words, children entering first grade should have formed a number concept of two or three objects. Much of the time allotted to the teaching of numbers in the first three grades is spent helping children to build up a number vocabulary to interpret terms found in arithmetic problems. The rate of their progress will depend to a large extent on the preparation they had prior to entering school.

Rhymes and Stories Add Meaning to Number Words

A child who has heard number words repeated in conversation, stories, and rhymes will have formed a stronger number concept than the parent realizes. It is not advisable, however, to teach him just how to say numbers; it is very possible for him to repeat numbers perfectly from one to one hundred without having learned anything about the relationship of one number to another. A child's daily routine offers many situations for him to gather information about numbers and their meaning. For example, when your child hears the nursery rhyme, "Rub-a-Dub-Dub, Three Men In a Tub" (volume I, page 48), he will see the picture of the three men in a tub at the same time he hears the word three mentioned in the rhyme. The word three will begin to take on meaning for him as he associates the word he hears with the picture he sees.

In the humorous New England ballad, "Old Noah" (volume I, page 112), he will hear many number phrases repeated, such as "There's one wide river to cross" and "The animals went in two by two, / The elephant and the kangaroo." Here again, as the child looks at the picture that tells of the "one wide river" and the "elephant and the kangaroo" going in "two by two," he will begin to associate the meaning of the words with the relationship between one and two. He sees that two is more than one, and likewise, that one is less than two.

In volume II, page 94, you will find another old favorite, "Ten Little Indians." In this rhyme children not only hear the names of the numbers from one to ten, but also learn the relationship of one number to another. They will enjoy the humor of the rhyme at the same time as they learn that ten little Indians are more than four or five little Indians. The illustrations will add appeal and help children form a concept for the numbers mentioned in the rhyme.

Counting-rhymes and counting-stories interest children and help give them a number vocabulary that they will use and understand. Children who have number words in their vocabulary will be able to express their ideas more accurately. In the story "The Three Trucks" (volume I, page 177), they will become familiar with the comparative terms big, little, and enormous, and begin using them in conversation.

Everyday Number Experiences

Play experiences offer children many opportunities to use their knowledge of numbers. The number experiences that come up naturally in children's days will be most meaningful to them. Let your child be responsible for counting the chairs, plates, and napkins needed for the family dinner. Let him discover the number of fingers and toes on his hands and feet, and the number of buttons on his sweater by counting them. Speak of his age and the number of pounds he weighs, and you will find him doing likewise. These are but a few experiences that will make numbers more meaningful to him. Encourage him to use comparative terms, such as big, little, enormous, oldest, youngest, and tallest when he needs them in conversation. Reading numbers on houses, automobile license plates, and the telephone dial; identifying coins as a penny, nickel, dime, or quarter; speaking of his gloves and shoes as a pair of gloves and a pair of shoes; and speaking of a dozen eggs, a pound of butter, or a quart of milk will add much to his understanding of numbers.

When your child is a little older, draw attention to the numbers on the pages of his books. When he is learning to read for himself, encourage him to use the index in the books to find specific stories. Dominoes and number and counting games where score keeping is required will tend to make his knowledge of numbers more practical and usable. Let him become familiar with the calendar and learn to speak of the days of the week and the names of the months. Draw his attention to the dates on letters, newspapers, and magazines, and the numbers on thermometers and clocks.

Children learn the value of measuring and planning when they are faced with the problem of making things fit. They learn to choose the correct size of paper or wood that will best suit their needs. In fact, it is amazing how quickly children learn to judge size and distance by looking and examining. Their conversation will become specific and accurate as number words seep into their vocabulary.

Your child's introduction to numbers will be pleasant or boring, meaningful or vague, according to the early experiences he is exposed to in the home before he goes to school. In the selections found in the first three volumes of *My Book House*, he will hear many words and phrases that will help him understand numbers, time, days of the week, seasons, and measures.

REFERENCES

Counting Rhymes. See index in *My Book House*, volume XII, page 253.

Also in *My Book House*, volume I:

* "Diddle, Diddle, Dumpling," page 37
* "Old King Cole," page 44
* "Rub-a-Dub-Dub," page 48
* "There Were Two Blackbirds," page 51
* "Three Little Kittens," page 53
* "There Were Two Little Boys," page 74
* "Engine, Engine Number Nine," page 85

* "Here Come Three Jolly, Jolly Sailor Boys," page 96
* "Three Old Maids a-Skating Went," page 110
* "There Were Three Duckies," page 127
* "Mary Milks the Cow," page 35
* "The Children and the Bear," page 206

Stories with number references in *My Book House*, volume II and III:

* "Reen-Reens-Reeny Croak Frog," page 37
* "Two Birds and Their Nest," page 45
* "The Little Rabbit Who Wanted Red Wings," page 87
* "Noah's Ark," page 101

* "The Tale of Peter Rabbit," page 112
* "Rama and the Tigers," page 118
* "The Village of Cream Puffs," page 124
* "The Adventures of a Water Baby," page 211

See also Counting and Number Experiences in various charts in chapter 15 of this book. Typical references to number words and comparative terms appearing in the reading readiness tests will be found in sections of *My Book House* listed below.

THREE

* "Old King Cole," volume I, page 44
* "Three Little Kittens," volume I, page 53
* "The Three Trucks," volume I, page 177
* "Johnny and the Three Goats," volume II, page 47
* "Goldilocks and the Three Bears," volume III, page 20

FIVE

* "Dame Durden," volume I, page 58
* "Five Little Chicks," volume I, page 64
* "Over in the Meadow," volume I, page 138
* "Ten Little Indians," volume I, page 94

TALL

* "Biting Marion," volume I, page 174
* "The Little Red Hen and the Grain of Wheat," volume II, page 13
* "Ole Shut-Eyes, the Sandman," volume II, page 26
* "Whisky Frisky," volume II, page 82
* "The Tale of Nutcracker," volume II, page 218

You don't buy character. . . you build it!

The quality of character that makes for greatness doesn't come "ready made." It must be built! And that building must start during the years before your child goes to school. It is then that his character is being shaped by everything he sees, hears, reads, and is exposed to.

The Three R's

READY TO READ

READY FOR SCHOOL

READY FOR LIFE

As young children observe their parents reading and hear rhymes and simple stories, a desire for reading begins. With My Book House, reading readiness develops easily and naturally. When you show him the interesting pictures, read to him the rhymes and stories especially fitted to his level of understanding, he learns to look to good books as an active source of pleasure. He is then eager to learn to read for himself.

Here, again, readiness is an emotional conditioning—a joyous anticipation of new experiences, new interests, new associations. My Book House will prepare your child to approach school with confidence. It will help him express his ideas more clearly, and to better make the adjustments required by a new school environment.

Good habits of mind and character are the sound basis for a happy and successful life. With the aid of My Book House you will find a very effective way to encourage these desirable qualities. Thus equipped, your child will be prepared to use his talents and abilities to contribute something worthwhile to the world.

*P*arents ask, "What must we do to have our children fully ready for school?"

12

Readiness for Grades One, Two, and Three

PSYCHOLOGISTS AND EDUCATORS have set the first three grades in school as the readiness period for reading. Learning to read, they agree, should be determined by a child's physical, mental, social, and emotional maturity. The experiences she has in the home during the preschool years will determine your child's readiness for the learning expected of her. Wise parents will plan to encourage the child's natural development and readiness for learning from infancy to school age. And they will not forget that a child's introduction to reading must be approached with patience and understanding. Connecting a sound with a few odd-looking letters is hard; connecting an idea with a sound is also hard. Yet children must learn both of these difficult things.

Parents are constantly asking, "What can we do to help our child in these early years?" Perhaps this question can best be answered by examining the reason educators give for failure in the primary grades.

Causes of Failure in the First Three Grades

- Inadequate preparation in the home.
- Very small vocabulary.
- Inability to pay attention.
- Entering school with insufficient story background.
- Lack of desire to read.

Qualities That Make for Readiness for Learning and Reading in the First Three Grades

Qualities of readiness must be developed gradually over a period of time. For a child to be ready to learn, she must be able to do the following:

Listen and pay attention The habit of listening and paying attention should begin in the first months of a baby's life, and her ability to listen, pay attention, and concentrate will grow from year to year. Learning to listen and pay attention are basic to your child's readiness for learning. Carefully age-graded rhymes, poems, stories, and pictures will appeal to her and make her want to listen and pay attention.

Reproduce stories in her own words The child must hear a variety of rhymes, poems, and stories over and over before she has a desire to retell them. These stories should be written in short well-knit sentences and in a vocabulary suited to her needs. Up until five, most children are not interested in plots. Stories like "First Adventures" (volume I, page 160) and "The Three Trucks" (volume I, page 177) are typical experience stories that encourage retelling. Selections with repetitive qualities such as "Over in the Meadow" (volume I, page 138), "The Little Gray Pony" (volume II, page 17), and "The Gingerbread Man" (volume II, page 58) invite children to repeat familiar parts.

Observe details in objects and pictures Throughout *My Book House*, beautiful illustrations, accurate in every detail, add to the child's enjoyment and give her the necessary preschool preparation. The little boy in "Little Jack

Horner" (volume I, page 48) actually sits in the corner, and younger children can easily tell from the picture illustrating "Rub-a-Dub-Dub" (volume I, page 48) which is the butcher and which is the baker. Children depend on pictures to understand the meaning of stories, and it is important that the illustrations in their first books be accurate. Pictures help children build up the sound and meaning of many new words. For example, the poem at the top of page 86 in volume I begins with

> *Star light, star bright,*
> *Very first star I've seen tonight;*

and deals with one star; the illustration accompanying it emphasizes this thought with one star pictured in the sky. The second poem begins with

> *Many, many stars are in the skies*
> *As old, as old as Adam;*

and emphasizes the phrase "many stars," so the illustration accompanying it shows the sky filled with stars. The words of these poems and the illustrations belong together and help children see what they hear and read. In this way they build concepts of the new words and are unconsciously being prepared for reading.

Express ideas and share them with a group To do this children must be able to enunciate relatively clearly and have an adequate working vocabulary. The child who is familiar with the selections in the first three volumes in *My Book House* has been exposed to 6,800 different words used over and over again to express a variety of ideas.

Understand and use comparative terms A story background will help your child develop her ability along this line. *My Book House* provides for this phase of her development by including hundreds of comparative terms like these:

big, little, enormous	dark, light
fast, slow	cool, warm
near, far	more than, less than

Follow directions Children with a good understanding and speaking vocabulary are equipped to understand and follow directions with ease and confidence. *My Book House* helps your child to build an understanding and speaking vocabulary and form the habit of listening and paying attention.

Long stories may be too complicated for young children. The stories they hear in their preschool years must be free from complicated plots, and the language and sentence structure must be simple enough to make them want to use the words and phrases in their own daily speech. Stories will help your child mature more fully at each age level, so they should cover a variety of childhood interests. Parents should not choose, for instance, only animal or train stories; they should expose their child to rhymes, poems, stories of everyday activities, nature, community interests, the Bible, wholesome adventure and imaginative interests, as well as stories of people from other lands. Carefully age-graded stories suggest desirable social qualities children may accept as their own. They help children to make decisions of their own and gain a better understanding of honesty, truth, kindness, and courtesy. See various charts in chapter 15 of this book.

Reading Difficulties in Primary Grades

Limited story and language experiences may cause reading failures. Do not overlook the value of a story background to encourage your child's readiness for learning. She will never forget the stories you have taken the time to read to her through the years, and she will treasure the memory of the person who read to them to her. If your want to stimulate your child's desire to read for herself, make story time a happy, intimate experience in her day.

Learning Disabilities*

If your child is having problems achieving at her expected age and ability level in school, she may have a learning disability. Academic difficulties due

*Learning disabilities material derived from *A to Z Guide to Your Children's Behavior.* Compiled by the Children's National Medical Center under the direction of David Mrazek and William Garrison with Laura Elliott (pages 164-167). © 1993 by the Children's National Medical Center. A Perigee Book, The Putnam Berkley Group.

to learning disabilities tend to show up in the early school years, so it is wise to have your child assessed if she is not succeeding in school despite obvious effort. There are three general types of learning disabilities—those in reading, writing, and mathematics. If you suspect your child has one, seek help from the school's counselor or administrators in getting your child tested. Your child's teacher should be made aware of her difficulty so that he or she can help her as much as possible. Depending on the nature and severity of the child's difficulty, she may be placed in classes designed to help her develop strategies to deal with her particular learning difficulty or you might seek the help of a trained tutor. Children with learning disabilities are found to have average or above average intelligence quotients when tested, so the disability is no reflection of their intelligence. Yet if children have a learning problem and are not aware of it, they may begin to feel that they are not as smart as others and begin to feel bad about themselves. Moreover, those with learning disabilities might not understand verbal communications correctly and thus experience interpersonal difficulties with teachers and fellow students. Research indicates that learning disabilities have a physiological basis and run in families, but no specific underpinning has been identified.

_____

*The Alphabet Equals the Wheel**

Anyone who stops for a moment can hardly help seeing the rightness of the phonic mode of entry into the complexities of the written word. It is precisely because the spelling of nearly all languages is liable to many vagaries that mastery of the phonetic alphabet gives the comfort of a solid base for the mass of words that follow the rule. And the words that do not can at least be approximated. A simple anecdote makes the point: in the corridor of the elementary school the artwork of the first and second grades was posted—a vivid display of color and line. In the corner of one painting the viewer could read: for mrs. Wilsn. The young artist had had no occasion to see her teacher's name written, and under the regime of look-and-say she would never have had the remotest idea of its "look," for names would not be taught. But with sounded letters, all on her own, she was able to write her dedication unmistakably.

The lesson is plain. Children want to know how. Teaching helps to learn how when able people teach. But they must be allowed to do it, with guidance and encouragement as needed, and with the least amount of dictation from outside. Teaching is a demanding, often back-breaking job; it should not be done with the energy left over after meetings and pointless paperwork have drained hope and faith in the enterprise. Accountability, the latest cure in vogue, is to be looked for only in results. Good teaching is usually well-known to all concerned without questionnaires or approved lesson plans. The number of good teachers who are now shackled by bureaucratic obligations to superiors who know little or nothing about the classroom cannot even be guessed at. They deserve from an Education President an Emancipation Proclamation.

The gain would not be theirs alone. When good teachers perform and pupils learn, the sense of accomplishment produces a momentum that light-

_____

*Excerpt from Jacques Barzun. "The Alphabet Equals the Wheel" in *Begin Here: The Forgotten Conditions of Teaching and Learning,* (pages 18–19). © 1991 by The University of Chicago. Reprinted by permission of The University of Chicago Press.

ens the toil for both. Discipline is easier to maintain, and failures become exceptions instead of the rule. As a further result there is no need for the fiddling and innovating, the "crash programs," all with more special funding and still more reports and evaluations and assessments. Since the millions go chiefly into new bureaus, new manuals full of "guidelines," and new textbooks that make only the publishers happy, the savings can be great. The taxpayers themselves benefit from a school that works.

As your child's reading interests broaden, you can help guide him in his choice of reading.

13

When Children
Read for Themselves—
Grades Four, Five, and Six

Bʏ ᴛʜᴇ ᴛɪᴍᴇ children enter fourth grade, schools expect them to have learned the basic techniques of reading and to be able to read simple stories and essays with ease and pleasure.

It is usually at about this time in a child's development that many parents lose contact with their child's reading interests, and yet, although children have learned to read fairly well by this time, children still need your help in selecting their reading. Their interests have grown in leaps and bounds, and their quest for information has frequently grown beyond their own reading ability. It is wise to use this opportunity to guide your child's choice of reading so that he will continue to choose reading for recreation and pleasure.

Choose Material on Children's Level of Understanding

Children of nine or ten frequently have difficulty finding interesting and satisfying reading material outside the schoolroom. If they are left to struggle with reading material that is too difficult, they may lose interest in it and look upon it as a necessary evil for study in school.

You will find *My Book House* a valuable aid in guiding your child's choice of reading during this transitional stage. It will give him interesting and enjoyable reading in his own home. And, what is most important, the selections he reads will be age-graded to suit his reading ability as well as his interests. He will become familiar with the work of outstanding poets and identify selections as belonging to certain periods in the history of literature. He will be exposed to a balanced variety of reading material including stories from the Bible, selections from Shakespeare and Chaucer, and outstanding characters in history, science, and the arts. The selections he reads will develop his appreciation of good literature and make him more discriminating in his reading. The notes at the bottom of the pages in *My Book House* volumes suggest additional books for him to read.

In *My Book House* your child will have the opportunity to read selections from the literature of the world and gain valuable information he can relate to the facts of history, geography, and social science that he is learning in school. He will gather ideas that will add interest and life to his studies. A child's love for adventure is high during this period, and *My Book House* selections will provide him with tales of heroes and adventurers who have contributed to our civilization. During this period your child's social behavior and choice of language will reflect his attempt to imitate the people he admires. The characters he meets in his reading will unconsciously influence his own emotional reactions and social behavior.

What do you mean Bobby will be given a <u>readiness test?</u>

Too many parents fail to realize,
until too late, that children must be ready to enter school.
Nine out of ten schools now give a
readiness test when children enter first grade to
determine if he is prepared for school work.

How will your child rate?

Daily use of

My Book House

will build school

readiness

The child's appreciation of literature develops gradually from early childhood through adolescence.

14

Reading in
the Upper Grades

READING MUST PROVIDE pleasure, relaxation, and growth to satisfy the
boy or girl in the upper grade and junior high school. Children's capacity for
understanding what they read and their ability to read fluently grow with
each new reading and personal experience. During these years, their appreciation for literature and quest for pleasurable and discriminating reading will
depend upon the background of stories parents and teachers give them.

The process of learning to read goes on for several years. The child is now
developing new emotional patterns and may have periods of boredom. This
is an opportunity for parents to remind their child that books and stories can
be fun and joyful. You should take an active interest in your child's reading,
and the reading hour can take on a new reason for being. Teachers and librar-
ians agree that parents who read with their child during these years are
actively cooperating with the school in building up a love of reading and
increasing their child's chances of becoming a good reader. Busy parents who
feel they don't have time to read to their grade school child might recall the

lines of the poem by Strickland Gillilan, "Richer than I you can never be; / I had a mother who read to me."

Remember that your child's success in many school subjects is based on her ability to read. And her enjoyment of reading depends greatly on whether the literature she is exposed to stirs her emotions and portrays life in a way that enables her to link it with her own. It should have the kind of literary excellence that enables the child to experience vicariously the author's reactions, and it should have the effect of making the characters—both fictional and real—so vitally interesting to her that their personalities and experiences will enrich your child's thoughts and ideas.

Share Your Child's Reading Interests

The child's appreciation of literature develops gradually from early childhood through adolescence. Take advantage of every opportunity to share in your child's reading activities. The parent who reads certain exciting chapters and outstanding scenes aloud will add pleasure and interest to the child's reading and encourage her to read the selections for herself.

Reading Influences Personality Development

The style of literature your child comes in contact with will influence her personality, conversation, and attempts at writing. Abraham Lincoln is just one example of the influence of reading in the formation of style, character, and personality. The Bible was the dominant source of his reading. Lincoln's speeches and addresses reflect the simplicity, directness, and appeal of the Bible.

These are the years for your boy or girl to meet Dickens, Clemens, Hawthorne, Irving, Shakespeare, and other fine literary personalities. Biographies that trace the human struggles and conflicts of artists, musicians, authors, explorers, statesmen, and scientists will inspire and encourage the adolescent to read widely. Bible and hero stories, tales of chivalry, adventure, and romance also have strong appeal. At this age, children are interested in dramatization and making scenery and costumes for plays; they may read avidly for details to help reproduce the stories realistically.

Importance of Varied Reading

During the later school years children are called upon to do many types of reading. They must know how to skim for facts, read in detail for description, be able to pick essential points, and be able to evaluate what they have read. A varied background of reading will tend to make them more efficient in their studies. Isolated facts are not as meaningful or retained as easily as information they glean from authentic story material. The story elements place facts in their context setting, making them more appealing and meaningful. Also, do not overlook the need for poetry and prose at this age, as the musical sounds of words hold particular charm for the adolescent.

A wide variety of selections from the literature of the world are listed in the index of *My Book House*, volume XII, under the following headings:

* Bible Selections, page 251
* Biographical Sketches, page 251
* Fables, page 260
* Fairy Tales and Poems, page 260

* Folklore and Legends, page 262
* Hero and Heroine Stories, page 264
* Humorous Rhymes and Stories, page 265

Children using this index will get valuable experience that will help them to classify the various periods in literature. They will learn to associate authors, poets, and playwrights with their various countries, time periods, and literary groups.

See also various charts in chapter 15 of this book.

Both home and school aims need to be coordinated if children are to enjoy a full life.

15

Home-School Coordinating Charts

T HE CHARTS on the following pages have been prepared for parents who are using *My Book House*. The first chart gives a comprehensive picture of the attitudes and qualities that must be developed in preschool children if they are to make a happy, successful adjustment to the new environment of the schoolroom. The charts list the material in *My Book House* that will help develop the necessary habits and attitudes in the child.

The next three charts reveal what many schools expect of children from the first grade through the upper grades and indicate where to find help in *My Book House Plan*. The general aims listed on these charts for each grade in school have been chosen after a careful review of the courses of study used in schools throughout the United States. With this information at hand, parents will be better equipped to understand their child's needs and offer intelligent guidance.

It is more important for parents to provide a home background that will enrich the child's experiences, stimulate his imagination, and arouse intellectual curiosity, than to drill him on the things he is learning in school or help him with his actual lessons. Play equipment; creative materials, such as clay, paint, and crayons; and carefully selected books in the home will encourage your child's natural readiness for learning. Your child's attitudes toward school reflect parental attitudes toward reading, learning, and problem-solving, just as his speech reflects the language he hears in the home.

The aim of both home and school should be coordinated if children are to enjoy a full life and make their adjustments happily and successfully.

Kindergarten

SOCIAL BEHAVIOR AND ADJUSTMENT QUALITIES

In school
your child is
expected to:

—show some self-control and self-dependence.
—courteous in speech and actions.
—appreciate the work of others.
—be relatively relaxed and at ease with the group.

To find
help:

—See chapters 5 and 16 of this book.
—See also selections listed in index of *My Book House*, volume XII, under: Ambition, Boastfulness, Cheerfulness, Consideration of Others, Cooperation, Courage, Courtesy, Faith, Honesty, and Obedience.
—Choose stories best suited to your child's needs and level of understanding.

LANGUAGE AND LITERATURE ACTIVITIES

In school
your child is
expected to:

—retell short stories and learn rhyme and imaginative play.
—create stories and poems.
—engage in dramatic and imaginative play.
—share ideas with others and contribute to group discussions.
—speak comprehensibly and enunciate clearly.
—follow directions and understand the language of the classroom.

To find
help:

—See chapters 2, 3, and 4 of this book.
—*My Book House* selections stimulate children's desire to retell their story experiences and to share their ideas with others. They also encourage the love of good language and give children language patterns they unconsciously imitate in their own conversation.

—Stories about everyday happenings expose children to short well-knit sentences to use in their own speech.

—See selections listed in index of *My Book House*, volume XII, under: Animals, Birds, Boats, City, Farm and Country, Holidays, Humorous Rhymes and Stories, Lullabies, Mother Goose, Nature, and Seasons.

Repetitive selections

—Volume I, pages 33, 38, 102, 100, 112, 114, 126, 138, 160, etc.

—Volume II, pages 13, 17, 47, 52, 58, 118, 145, 192, 200, and 209.

—Volume III, pages 76, 85, 99, and 111.

—The colorful accurate pictures accompanying the selections in *My Book House* help children to see what they hear and to build concepts of meaning for new words.

—Children in kindergarten are expected to have an understanding vocabulary of about 6,500 words. In the selections for the first three volumes of *My Book House*, they hear over 6,800 different words that will help enrich their vocabulary.

CREATIVE EXPRESSION

In school your child is expected to

—experiment with scissors, paper, paste, clay, paint, wood, cloth, crayons, etc.

—constructively use sand, blocks, playground equipment, etc.

—be imaginative and to express a variety of ideas with creative materials.

—choose their own activities and have a desire to reproduce individual experiences.

—be resourceful in using materials.

—recognize and name colors.

To find
help:
—See chapters 17 and 18 of this book.

—Colorful pictures throughout *My Book House* make children conscious of color. Names of colors are mentioned in rhymes and stories to connect them with the pictures. (There are nearly 200 references to color in the first three volumes alone.)

—Color words are emphasized in the following sampling of selections in *My Book House*:

—Volume I, pages 18, 20, 24, 25, 28, 29, 30, 33, 35, 37, and 41

—Volume II, pages 13, 17, 23, 24, 26. 30, 33, 35, 37, 40, 41, and 45

COUNTING AND NUMBER EXPERIENCES

In school
your child is
expected to:
—use numbers in work and play.

—include number words in vocabulary when needed.

—be able to count to 10 and know something of the relationship of one number to another.

To find
help:
—See chapter 11 of this book.

—*My Book House* contains over 175 selections that include number and comparative terms to help children build a concept of meaning for numbers and their relationships.

—The accurate pictures illustrating counting rhymes and stories help children build a meaningful concept of numbers from 1 to 10, e.g., "Over in the Meadow" (volume I, page 138) and "Ten Little Indians" (volume II, page 94). See also Counting Rhymes in *My Book House* index, volume XII, page 253.

NATURE EXPERIENCES AND SOCIAL SCIENCE

*In school
your child is
expected to:*
—be conscious of beauty and happenings in nature.
—be kind and considerate in care of pets and birds.
—learn farm animals and how they help man.
—learn how sun, moon, wind, rain, and snow help man.
—recognize and speak of living creatures in their environment, such as birds, animals, and insects
—understand the farmer's contribution toward feeding and
clothing society.

*To find
help:*
See chapter 10 of this book.
—There are over 500 selections in *My Book House* to
awaken your child's interest in nature.
—See selections listed in index of *My Book House*, volume
XII, under Nature, page 270. (Listed are 125 animal
selections, including 50 of birds alone.)

DESIRABLE WORK HABITS

*In school
your child is
expected to:*
—be able to work toward a goal and find satisfaction in their
own achievements.
—be able to concentrate and have an attention span of about
15 minutes.
—complete work.
—be able to work alone and with others.
—choose materials best suited for their needs.
—be able to take care of materials and use them
constructively.

*To find
help:*
—See chapters 5 and 17 of this book.
—See selections listed in index of *My Book House*, volume
XII, under: Cheerfulness, Cooperation, Crying and
Whining, Industry, Perseverance, and Self-Reliance.
—Choose selections best suited to your child's needs and
level of understanding.

MUSIC

In school
your child is
expected to:

—match tones and sing simple melodies.
—march, skip, hop, and jump in rhythmic fashion.
—reproduce simple rhythm on drum, tambourine, rhythm sticks, etc.

To find
help:

—See chapter 21 of this book.
—See selections listed under Music in index of *My Book House*, volume XII. Included in this list are stories and notes about more than 60 composers whose works date from the 17th century to the present, or Modern Period.
—Illustrations of musical instruments are listed in the index of *My Book House*, volume XII, page 269.
—Suggested stories and poems for kindergarten:
  Volume II, pages 17, 26, 40, 57, 80, 131, 150, 163, and 218.
  Volume III, pages 40, 61, and 110.

Grades One, Two, and Three

SOCIAL BEHAVIOR AND ADJUSTMENT QUALITIES

*In school
your child is
expected to:*

—be able to interact cooperatively and peacefully with others.

—be cooperative, considerate, and courteous.

—have pretty good emotional control.

—be helpful and friendly, and respect the property of others.

—be truthful and honest, and enjoy helping others.

—be eager, alert, observing, and able to initiate ideas.

—give and take constructive criticism.

—assume responsibility, to be resourceful and help himself.

*To find
help:*

—See chapter 5 of this book.

—See selections in index of *My Book House*, volume XII, under: Ambition, Boastfulness, Cheerfulness, Consideration of Others, Cooperation, Courage, Courtesy, Faith, Honesty, and Obedience.

—Choose selections best suited to your child's needs and level of understanding.

LANGUAGE AND LITERATURE ACTIVITIES

*In school
your child is
expected to:*

—retell stories in relatively well-knit sentences.

—develop pride in the use of good language.

—enunciate clearly and build an interesting vocabulary.

—understand the language of the schoolroom, follow directions, and share ideas with others.

—have a background of rhymes, stories, and poems.

—write original poems, riddles, and stories.

To find
help:

—See chapters 2, 3, 7, and 12 of this book.

—The balanced variety of carefully age-graded selections in *My Book House* stimulates children's desire to retell stories and experiences. They also suggest good language patterns, which children will use in their own conversation.

—The story language of the literature in *My Book House* builds children's appreciation for good speech. See index of My Book House, volume XII, for selections that will appeal to your child.

Repetitive
selections

—See reading chart on page 27 of this book.

—See also "Climbing the Ladder of Years"—pages 127 to 155 of this book.

CREATIVE EXPRESSION

In school
your child is
expected to:

—be able to use materials constructively and express ideas with blocks, clay, paper, wood, crayon, paint, scissors, cloth, etc.

—make puppet shows, puppets, stage scenery, costumes, posters, patterns, etc., for units of study, dramatic play, holidays, and gifts.

To find
help:

—See chapters 17 and 18 of this book.

—Throughout the twelve volumes of *My Book House* children will find suggestions and ideas to stimulate their desire to create.

COUNTING AND NUMBER EXPERIENCES

In school
your child is
expected to:

—build a concept of meaning for numbers and their relationship.

—count by 2s, 3s, 5s, and 10s.

—make change and identify coins—toy and real money.

—write numbers.

—read numbers on calendars, charts, timetables, pages of books, and in tables of contents of books.

—play games involving counting and score keeping.

—know the meaning of number terms—one dozen, half a dozen, pound, inch, foot, yard, length, height, width, circle, square, rectangle, triangle, pint, quart, gallon, cup, and glass.

—solve daily problems involving money and measuring.

—tell sizes of various items of clothing.

—use ruler: 1 inch markings in the 1st grade, 1/2 inch in 2nd grade, and 1/4 inch in 3rd grade.

To find help:

—See chapter 11 of this book.

—*My Book House* contains over 175 selections that include number and comparative terms to help children build a concept of meaning for numbers and their relationship.

—References to numbers are found in the following partial list of selections in *My Book House*:

Volume I, pages 19, 39, 43, 44, 47, 48, 49, 51, 53, 54, 55, 57, 58, 60, 100, 110, 112, 121, 135, 138, 156, 177, etc.

Volume II, pages 24, 33, 45, 47, 87, 94, 96, 101, 112, 118, 124, etc.

Volume III, pages 12, 20, 28, 76, 95, 110, 111, 129, 204, etc.

See also Counting Rhymes in index of *My Book House*, volume XII, page 253.

DESIRABLE WORK HABITS

In school your child is expected to:

—use materials and tools constructively.

—plan before acting, choose materials wisely, finish one job before starting another, and be orderly and neat.

—show initiative, resourcefulness, and pride in workmanship.

—assume responsibility toward work and feel the joy of accomplishment.

—concentrate, cooperate, and be courteous and helpful.

—appreciate and respect the work and skill of others.

—See chapter 5 of this book.

*To find
help:*
  —See selections listed in index of *My Book House*, volume
XII, under: Alertness, Cooperation, Crying and Whining,
Fair Play, Industry, Laziness, Perseverance, and Self-Reliance.
—Choose selections best suited to your child's needs and
level of understanding.

MUSIC

*In school
your child is
expected to:*
  —appreciate music and be able to express themselves in song.
—learn about time, notes, and tone value.
—listen to music and identify two or three instruments.
—recognize at least six compositions and name the artists.
—make simple homemade instruments, learn the scale, and
create simple, original tunes.

*To find
help:*
  —See chapter 21 of this book.
—See selections listed under Music in index of *My Book
House*, volume XII, page 267. Included in this list are sto-
ries and notes about more than 60 composers whose
works date from the 17th century to the present, or
Modern Period.
—Illustrations of musical instruments are listed in the index
of *My Book House*, volume XII, page 269.
—Suggested reading for grades one, two, and three:
Volume II, pages 17, 40, 41, 57, 131, 143, 150, 180, and
218.
Volume III, pages 40, 61, 95, 110, 123, 134, 148, 151, and
170.
Volume IV, pages 73 and 159.
Volume V, page 222.

READING

*In school
your child is
expected to:*
  —enjoy reading and get ideas from the printed page.
—learn to sound new words and read aloud without too
much hesitancy before individual words.
—read poetry and prose orally.
—be able to locate simple passages in books of their own
reading ability.

—learn to grasp main ideas when reading silently.

—learn to sense a phrase or line before reading aloud.

—cover a great deal of easy reading material and seek outside reading to develop fluency.

—develop a reading vocabulary:

Grade One—from 5,000 to 6,000 words.

Grade Two—from 6,000 to 7,000 words.

Grade Three—from 7,000 to 8,000 words.

To find help:

—See chapter 12 of this book.

—Suggested reading for early school years. See selections listed in index of *My Book House*, volume XII, under: Animals, Birds, Boats, City, Experience Stories and Poems, Fables, Fairy Tales and Poems, Farm and Country, Folklore and Legends, Holidays, Humorous Rhymes and Stories, Insects, Lullabies, Mother Goose, Nature, and Seasons.

—Choose selections in *My Book House* best suited to your child's needs and level of understanding.

Repetitive selections:

—Volume I, pages 33, 38, 102, 110, 112, 114, 126, 138, 160, etc.

—Volume II, pages 13, 17, 47, 52, 58, 118, 145, 192, 200, and 209.

—Volume III, pages 76, 99, and 110.

—The selections in the first three volumes of *My Book House* bring children in contact with 6,800 different words to help them meet the 7,000 and 8,000 word reading vocabulary required of them in school at the end of the third grade.

NATURE EXPERIENCES AND SOCIAL SCIENCE

In school your child is expected to:

—appreciate nature and be observant of seasonal changes.

—build a concept of meaning for words found in nature and science reading—lake, river, ocean, hill, valley, mountain, climate, temperature, steam, electricity, etc.

—learn sources and uses of plants, trees, flowers, fruits, vegetables, and animals.

—classify animals as farm, wild, water, and domestic.

—learn about pets and birds, their care, etc.

—learn the parts the sun, moon, stars, rain, wind, and snow play in life.

—learn sources of food and clothing.

—learn about people's occupations.

—become familiar with people of the world through poems, stories, and pictures.

To find help:

—See chapter 10 of this book.

—There are over 500 selections in *My Book House* to awaken your child's interest, observation, and appreciation of birds, animals, and the beauty of nature. See selections listed in the index of *My Book House*, volume XII, under: Nature; Seasons (49 references listed); Lake, Mountain, River, Sea, etc.; Birds (51 species of birds are listed); Moon, Stars, Sun, Wind, etc.; Occupations (29 occupations are listed); and Countries of the World.

Grades Four, Five, and Six

SOCIAL BEHAVIOR

*In school
your child is
expected to:*
—make decisions and have ideas of right and wrong.
—respect authority and the rights of others.
—develop desirable social qualities such as cheerfulness,
   cooperation, courage, friendliness, generosity, gratitude,
   happiness, helpfulness, honesty, industry, kindness, leadership, perseverance, politeness, self-control, tolerance, trust-
   worthiness, and truthfulness.

*To find
help:*
—See chapter 5 of this book.
—See selections listed in index of *My Book House*, volume
   XII, under: Ambition, Consideration of Others,
   Cooperation, Courage, Courtesy, Faithfulness, Honesty,
   Industry, Perseverance, Self-Control, and Tolerance.
—Choose selections best suited to your child's needs and
   level of understanding.
—See list of *My Book House* selections for encouraging dra-
   matic play in your child—page 183 of this book.

MUSIC

*In school
your child is
expected to:*
—sing for enjoyment.
—read notes of the scale and sing two-part songs.
—develop an appreciation for many types of music through
   listening.
—learn about famous composers and their compositions.

*To find
help:*
—See selections listed under Music in index of *My Book
   House*, volume XII, page 267. Included in this list are stories and notes about more than 60 composers whose
   works date from the 17th century to the present, or
   Modern Period.

—Illustrations of musical instruments are listed in the index of *My Book House*, volume II, page 269.

—Suggested reading in *My Book House* for grades four, five, and six:

Volume II, pages 150 and 218

Volume IV, pages 73, 159, and 183

Volume V, pages 162 and 222

Volume VI, pages 18 and 59

Volume VII, pages 72 and 90

Volumes VIII, page 29

Volume X, page 98

—See "Climbing the Ladders of Years"—pages 127 to 155 of this book.

READING, LANGUAGE, AND LITERATURE ACTIVITIES

In school your child is expected to:

—read widely for enjoyment and entertainment.

—gain rich and varied experiences from extensive reading.

—develop fluent oral reading and rapid silent reading.

—follow printed directions and determine central ideas.

—use index, table of contents, dictionary, and reference books.

—scan informational reading material at a rapid rate and get the important date and topic information.

—dramatize and illustrate stories.

—do literary reading and social science reading.

—develop desirable study habits.

—gather a background of myths, legends, folk tales, etc., from reading materials.

—be able to outline and summarize.

—develop a reading vocabulary:

Grade Four—from 8,000 to 9,000 words.

Grade Five—from 9,000 to 10,000 words.

Grade Six—from 10,000 to 11,300 words.

*To find
help:*

—See chapter 13 of this book.

—For stories suitable for dramatization see list of *My Book House* selections on page 105 of this book.

—Children gain an extensive reading background from selections such as these found in *My Book House:*
Volume III, pages 176 and 211.
Volume IV, pages 57 and 211.
Volume V, page 33.
Volume VII, pages 20, 40, 48, 96, and 119.
Volume VIII, pages 143 and 172.
Volume IX, pages 7, 27, 66, 89, and 134.
Volume X, pages 44, 48, 79, and 98.
Volume XII, pages 118, 122, 135, 141, 147, and 205.

—*My Book House* provides unusual reading to share with friends and classmates.

—Each volume of *My Book House* has its own table of contents and the extensive index in volume XII includes cross-references to give children additional experience in locating selections.

—The story element running through selections helps impress important facts on children's minds and adds interest to their studies.

—*My Book House* selections introduce children to myths, legends, folklore, and biographies. See selections listed in index of *My Book House*, volume XII, under Biographical Sketches, Epics, Folklore and Legends, and Myths.

—Children come in contact with many new words in *My Book House* reading that will enrich their vocabulary.

SOCIAL SCIENCE

*In school
your child is
expected to:*

—study foreign countries.

—study the regions of the United States.

—develop a knowledge and appreciation of the relationship between man and environment.

—have the ability to interpret geographical materials.

—make murals and maps.

*To find
help:*

—See also selections listed in index of *My Book House*, volume XII, under: Countries of the World, Nature: and Transportation.

HISTORY

*In school
your child is
expected to:*

—develop ideals of patriotism and service.
—develop ability to think critically about social questions.
—learn about discoveries, exploration, and colonization.

*To find
help:*

—See selections dealing with heroes, patriots, and famous characters in history listed in index of *My Book House*, volume XII, under: Ambition, Countries of the World, Hero and Heroine Stories, and Patriotism.
—For reading in *My Book House* to build a history background:
Volume IV, pages 161, 183, and 213.
Volume V, pages 112, 113, and 129.
Volume VIII, page 82.

SCIENCE

*In school
your child is
expected to:*

—develop a scientific attitude.
—develop knowledge of how the world works physically.
—study units of animals, insects, plants, weather, and the universe.

*To find
help:*

—See chapter 10 of this book.
—See selections in *My Book House* touching on the discovery of steam, invention of steamboat, etc.
—Suggested reading:
Volumes V, pages 45, 48, and 66.
Volume VI, pages 154 and 184.
—See selections listed in index of *My Book House*, volume XII, under: Animals, Birds, Nature, and Seasons.

POETRY

In school
your child is
expected to:

—commit favorite poems to memory and read poetry for enjoyment.

—study incidental poems.

—be familiar with the poetry of certain famous poets.

To find
help:

—In *My Book House* children meet the poetry of Whittier, Emerson, Longfellow, Noyes, Browning, Shakespeare, Lindsay, Tennyson, Scott, Rosetti, Burns, Chaucer, etc., as well as psalms from the Bible.

—Suggested poetry for children in grades four, five, and six:
Volume I, pages 113, 118, 148, 181, 194, 216, and 218.
Volume II, pages 78, 79, 105, 140, 141, 152, and 163.
Volume III, pages 11, 25, 26, 28, 40, 61, 62, 127, 136, 150, 170, 196, and 197.
Volume IV, pages 11, 56, 103, 136, and 180.
Volume V, pages 66, 112, and 129.
Volume VI, pages 70, 96, 97, and 131.
Volume VII, pages 47, 71, 72, 74, and 95.
Volume VIII, pages 7, 36, 91, and 188.
Volume IX, pages 89 and 171.
Volume X, pages 19 and 79.
Volume XI, page 7.

—Foreign rhymes are listed under Countries of the World in index of *My Book House*, volume XII, page 253.

—See selections listed in index of *My Book House*, volume XII, under: Biographical Sketches, Countries of the World, Nature, and Transportation.

Grades Seven, Eight, and Nine

LITERATURE AND LANGUAGE ACTIVITIES

*In school
your child is
expected to:*

—gain increased enjoyment from reading and appreciate material read.

—increase reading ability and scope of reading and enrich vocabulary.

—have a broader horizon and appreciate description, humor, and character.

—read for information.

—write book reviews and give oral reports of books read outside the classroom.

—write dramatizations correlated with literature.

—read biographies and factual and travel tales.

—write compositions and descriptive paragraphs and strive for smoothness and originality.

—read early American literature, historic tales, Bible stories, romantic poetry, and medieval tales.

—develop an appreciation for poems.

—read narrative poetry.

*To find
help:*

—See chapter 14 of this book.

—In these grades children's outside reading should enrich their studies in school and give them a broader horizon. It should satisfy their craving for travel and adventure.

—Diversified reading in *My Book House*—tales with historical background, literature from Elizabethan and early American periods, Shakespeare's plays, stories of travel and adventure, Bible stories, and medieval tales—develops children's appreciation of literature and causes children to be more discriminating in their leisure reading. What they read now may affect the pleasure and value they get from advanced courses in literature and history.

—Increased reading ability and an enriched vocabulary will result from reading selections in *My Book House* listed below:

Volume I, pages 148, 149, and 209.

Volume II, pages 45 and 217.

Volume III, page 25.

Volume IV, page 183.

Volume V, pages 113 and 222.

Volume VI, pages 71 and 201.

Volume VII, pages 11, 71, 73, 173, 182, and 210.

Volume VIII, pages 18 and 189

Volume IX, pages 89, 129, 134, and 171.

Volume X, pages 8, 48, 54, 98, 108, 151, 165, 175, 188, 203, 217, and 228.

Volume XI, pages 8, 29, 49, 72, 90, 107, and 152.

Volume XII, pages 15, 30, 102, 122, 135, 143, 147, 154, 190, and 213.

—See also selections listed in index of *My Book House*, volume XII, under: Biographical Sketches, Epics, Folklore and Legends, and Hero and Heroine Stories.

—The stories in *My Book House* suggest ideas for dramatization and bring additional interest to your child's studies.

CITIZENSHIP

In school your child is expected to:

—live peaceably with others and to respect authority.

—develop qualities of courage, cooperation, honesty, industry, initiative, leadership, loyalty, perseverance, resourcefulness, and responsibility.

—take an active part in school activities such as student council, assembly programs, and safety and health committees.

—make decisions, act independently, and seek worthwhile companions.

—continue interest in hobbies.

—develop an understanding of ethnic groups other than their own.

—grow in intellectual curiosity.

—compete and match their skills with others of their own age.

To find
help:

—See chapter 5 of this book.

—*My Book House* supplies thrilling stories of heroes who can be safely imitated and admired. See selections listed under Hero and Heroine Stories in index of *My Book House*, volume XII, page 264.

—See also selections listed in index, volume XII, under: Ambition, Cheerfulness, Cooperation, Courage, Faith, Honesty, Patriotism, and Resourcefulness.

—See index of *My Book House*, volume XII, Countries of the World, page 253, for stories about people of all nationalities that will create a feeling of friendliness, and racial and ethnic tolerance. See also selections listed under Tolerance, in index, volume XII, page 298.

—*My Book House* supplies unusual reading material in the home which helps children with assembly programs and other school activities.

—*My Book House* includes selections which challenge children's thinking, increase their scope of knowledge, and help them feel adequate to meet real life situations. See selections listed under Biographical Sketches in index, volume XII, page 251.

SOCIAL STUDIES

In school
your child is
expected to:

—study the regions in our country.

—study other civilizations.

—study the contributions of individuals in science.

—study the stars, planets, and map-making.

—help understand and interpret facts of their own environment—weather, heat, light, electricity, magnetism, stars, rocks, soil, and nature.

—learn about food, care of the body, and health.

To find
help:

—Suggested reading for grades seven, eight, and nine:
Volume IV, page 80.
Volume V, pages 113, 118, and 132.
Volume VII, page 26.

Volume VIII, pages 8, 36, 82, and 172.
Volume IX, pages 7, 27, 41, 66, 72, and 78.
Volume X, pages 21, 30, 44, 79, and 130.
Volume XI, pages 172, 173, and 216.
Volume XII, pages 45, 60, 70, and 190.
—See selections listed in index of *My Book House*, volume XII, under: Countries of the World and Nature.

MUSIC

In school your child is expected to:

—sing for enjoyment.
—develop an appreciation of music and to impart musical facts.
—learn about different styles of music.
—learn about the great composers and their music.
—arrange programs for special occasions.
—develop an interest in playing instruments.

To find help:

—See chapter 21 of this book.
—See selections listed under Music index of *My Book House,* volume XII, page 267. Included in this list are notes about more than 60 composers whose works date from the 17th century to the present, or Modern Period.
—Illustrations of musical instruments are listed in the index of My Book House, volume XII, page 269.
—Suggested reading in *My Book House* for grades seven, eight, and nine:
Volume V, page 222 (Note).
Volume VI, page 159.
Volume VII, page 72 (Note).
Volume VIII, pages 18 and 188 (Note).
Volume IX, pages 134 (Note) and 151 (Note).
Volume X, pages 11 (Note), 45 (Note), 98 (Note), 119 (Note), 154 (Note), 165 (Note), and 203 (Note).
Volume XI, page 73.

The Book House Plan is graded at the child's own rate of speed.

It enables you as a parent to open the door to your child's inner world and walk hand in hand with your child through the years in happy and understanding companionship.

16

Climbing the
Ladder of Years

By Martin L. Reymert
Founder and for many years Director of
The Mooseheart Laboratory for Child Research

Climbing the ladder of years is a valuable year-by-year guide prepared especially for *My Book House* by this internationally-known child psychologist. It is presented in a series of articles covering the outstanding phases in your child's physical, mental, emotional, social, and personality development from birth through early adolescence, and it is based on scientific research and personal observation of thousands of children. *My Book House Plan* offers this series as a guide to help reveal to parents the reactions and development they can expect of the average child.

Help your child mature fully at each age level and set her standards in accordance with her mental maturity. Many children fail only because they are exposed to situations they are unable to adequately deal with at that particular time. "Climbing the Ladder of Years" will help you stay in close touch with the things to expect from your child as she grows and develops. Avoid pushing her beyond her level of understanding, and she will experience the thrill of success and accomplishment rather than failure and discouragement.

In making use of these standards and steps of development, it should always be kept in mind that individual children differ from one another and may differ from these standards. Thoughtful parents, then, should not be over-anxious if their child does not conform to these standards exactly. When actually measured, each child has her own rate of development. Her mental development may be at one level, her social development at another, and her physical development at still another.

These standards should be seen as general guidelines of average development and should not be interpreted as rigid demands on any individual child.

Your Child's First Year

The Budding of Life

W HEN A CHILD is born we have a human being the exact like of which has never existed in the world's history and never will exist in the future. What we call "character and personality" is the product of the child's natural inborn tendencies interacting with her environment. We as parents, then, must realize our tremendous responsibility. One can honestly say that there is no more important responsibility in life than that of parenthood.

What we think of as "intelligence" has its earliest roots in the child's initial experiences in the world, such as when she is learning to control her body, or learning to react to people as social beings. Learning across all realms truly begins at birth. Social reactions are apparent in the infant at just a few weeks of age when she stops crying at the sound of mother's voice. By the end of the first month, the baby has a number of sounds that communicate to parents whether she is content or uncomfortable. Before there is an understanding of words or phrases, she will laugh and gurgle as answer to a playful frolicsome tone. So, from the start, parents should recognize the need for watching their tone of voice in speech and later in reading aloud.

While actions such as those of eye and hand movement grow more complex and coordinated, one of the fundamentals of intelligence—memory— begins to increasingly show itself during the second half of the first year. The baby smiles and laughs at the very sight of food; she laughs when her clothes are put on to go out. She begins to perceive relationships. For instance, if she drops something, she knows to look on the floor for it; if a block is out of reach, she pulls the table cover to bring it to herself. At the end of the first year, she begins to try imitating the words and actions of others. She is especially fond of definite rhythmic sounds in either music or nursery rhymes, and at this time, parents can help the child become fond of well-modulated voices in conversation and reading. The child is now quite social, using sounds and perhaps single words to get attention.

Thus, by the end of the first year, the child is using many of the basic components of intelligence and understanding. She will have developed characteristic habits of dealing with objects, of self-expression, and of reacting to other human beings.

Your Child's Second Year

12 to 18 Months

AT THIS TIME, your child literally crosses the threshold of a new world. From her first few faltering steps, she learns to walk. While the world before had to come to her, now she can go to it. She will run around for the sheer joy of running; she will open drawers and cabinets. She is now exploring her world.

She now begins to get more definite experiences of success and failure which will affect her character and personality. Her character and temperament will become more and more apparent and be influenced in many ways. If she cannot open a drawer or if she climbs and falls, she may meet these situations with either a temper tantrum or a persistent try-and-try-again. Her behavior is often so characteristic already in this early stage that she may be labeled, for instance, "stubborn and persistent" or "placid and easygoing." For information on temperament and personality, see chapter 5 of this book.

Now, too, she makes her first real use of language. While most of her words may still be incomprehensible to adults, she now uses her few words to actually communicate ideas. She learns to let her parents know that she wants to eat, or wants water.

She is gaining in self-assurance and self-control. Her memory span is longer. She recalls where she put things and what her parents do not want her to do, and she relates one experience to another. She expresses much of her understanding by imitation, and she is extremely interested in all things going on.

Whereas in the first year she was only beginning to recognize the form of things and to pay little attention to her own crayon scribblings on paper, these "pictures" are no longer mere blotches to her but take on meaning. She points to the picture of the "kitty," a "boy," "house," or "car." Nursery rhymes, jingles, and simple musical themes enthrall her. The book is more than an object to hold, it has something in it to look at!

Now the parents, through their own play with the child, have an opportunity to greatly enhance the development of her rapid steps in learning. The child's days should be well-ordered; she should have definite play periods with parents and family, but should also learn to amuse herself while alone. It is good to have things around that are suitable to the activities she is capable of at this age.

Your Child's Second Year

18 to 24 Months

As WE FOLLOW the youngster through her day, we find her walking upstairs without assistance, stopping with both feet on each step, still having great difficulty in making sudden stops or in changing her direction without losing her balance. She pulls off her socks herself, carries familiar objects from place to place, drinks from a cup, eats from a spoon, and knows an apple can be eaten but a block cannot. She no longer just throws her blocks around but can build a simple tower.

She can point to parts of her body upon request. She has what psychologists call quite an extensive "picture-vocabulary." If shown pictures of simple objects like a clock, scissors, basket, table, or house, she can name them. Your child's world at this time can be greatly expanded by an intelligent and systematic use of interesting pictures suited to her interests and capacities. Since primitive man's scribblings on the rocks, pictures have always been a most valuable means of imparting information and knowledge. The stimulation by parents or other family members by combining appropriate pictures with words will greatly aid her growing vocabulary.

The child now likes to talk to herself or others even when she obviously has nothing to say. She chatters with her newly found words much as she formerly gurgled in their crib. At the end of the second year, children have an average vocabulary of 900 words. Their words are mostly names of things, persons, actions, and situations. They are beginning to use words such as "me," "my," and "it" showing that they identify themselves as distinct from others. Here, it should be remembered that normal children vary widely in their rate of development.

Children at this age are fond of rhythms and like to hum and sing. Reading aloud suitable nursery rhymes combined with well-executed pictures of persons, things, and actions is increasingly valuable as it may be gradually grasped by your child. She is using simple sentences, sing-songy in rhythm, and sound patterns which mark the primitive stages of music and poetry. At this age she will start smiling in recognition when she hears the same nursery rhyme over and over again. Not only does the child profit by this repetition, but she actually likes and appreciates it.

Her emotional life is broadened; she shows spontaneous affection, signs of pity, sympathy, modesty, and shame. She pouts when scolded, smiles when praised, and shows evidence of guilt when she breaks things and may hang her head in disgrace. She is still very self-centered and rather content to be occupied all by herself. She is, however, becoming conscious of the family group, possibly hiding her toys from others, doing simple domestic tasks such as bringing various things to you, or showing her toys and things to others. Much of this is pure imitation, but some of it also expresses her reactions to definite situations and relationships.

Your Child's Third Year

Moving around quite freely now, the child learns more and more to cope with his environment, trying to change it to suit himself and trying to understand it. He is continuously investigating and exploring. He notices plants growing and the cat and dog jumping, sleeping, eating, and behaving in various ways. He experiences sickness and recovery in himself and others. He notices rain, thunder, and lightning; snow and sunshine; the change of seasons; and the moon and stars. He meets up with different temperaments in the family group, and in beginning preschool, he tumbles up against new personalities of children a little older and a little younger than himself.

Naturally, his curiosity grows in leaps and bounds and he is capable of questioning all around him, formulating small sentences, and increasing his vocabulary to some 1,500 words by the end of the third year. He is now building a definite vocabulary for social understanding and wants to "help" in everything that the family does. He likes to imitate people so that he can use words and talk. There are questions galore about everything, and he asks the same ones over and over again, such as "Why does it rain?" "Where does the sun go?" "What makes the car go?" "Do you love me?" Such questions should be intelligently answered by parents. Their repetition means the child is groping for knowledge and security. Naturally, some of his experiences may evoke fears if parents do not give proper explanations concerning what to fear and what not to fear.

Stories now hold his interest and keep him absorbed more than they did previously. He likes to hear the new words and to grasp meaning from them. He will retell stories, keeping the book before him as if he actually reads. He wants to hear the same story time and time again and will correct the reader if any changes in wording are introduced. The child's ideas and experiences can be greatly expanded at this time by intelligent reading material and pictures.

In his personal habits, he can wash his hands unaided and button his coat. He walks the stairs one foot to each step and wants to help with house-

hold tasks. He now clearly expresses jealousy and anger, and might have brief temper tantrums. He knows what is allowed and what is forbidden.

Parents must be patient but firm with talkative and constantly questioning children of three to four years. We should be aware that he needs to be shown attention and affection to give him a feeling of security. We should help him when he needs it, but let him do what he can for himself so that he may develop self-assurance and self-reliance.

Your child will probably have started to develop an interest in television if you have one in your house, especially if parents or siblings watch a lot of it.* Does television viewing lead to aggression, obesity, laziness, less reading and conversation? The answer seems to depend on what programs and how much television children are allowed to watch. Studies indicate that immedi-

---

*Television viewing material derived from *A to Z Guide to Your Children's Behavior*. Compiled by the Children's National Medical Center under the direction of David Mrazek and William Garrison with Laura Elliot (pages 288–290). ©1993 by the Children's National Medical Center. A Perigee book, The Putnam Berkley Group.

ately after watching a violent television show, violence in children's play increases; however, this quickly lessens in most children, except for those who have a history of aggressive play. It also appears that watching filmed violent aggressive acts on the news can make some children anxious and worried. Finally, bad eating habits such as binging without thinking in front of the television can increase the odds of obesity.

So should parents ban television? Well, that is a personal choice, but it is recommended that parents simply limit their child's viewing time and the programs he can watch. Television also has a lot of valuable educational programs, such as *Sesame Street* and *Mr. Rogers' Neighborhood*, which actually help improve a child's school readiness. In addition, there are various documentaries and nature programs that are well worth watching. It is recommended that as children grow, you limit their viewing not by amount of time but by program topic. In this way you promote the attitude of watching television when programs are worthwhile and not simply out of habit. Finally, it is recommended that you regularly watch certain programs with your child. This allows you to explain things to him, and as he grows older, to be able to bring up social or political issues for discussion, which may be particularly helpful in adolescence when many "sticky" issues may need to be discussed.

────────────

Your Child's Fourth Year

SHE IS NOW a better runner. Instead of being able to jump only up and down, she can now make a broadjump, both running and standing, and she likes to try different kinds of stunts. She is also better at doing things that require fine motor coordination, such as buttoning her clothing and lacing her shoes.

In her fourth year your child will be intellectually busy with many things, but not really absorbed in any one thing in particular. Her frequent questioning and talking seem to provide practice needed to improve her enunciation and increase her fluency. While she doesn't like to repeat things, she can carry on long conversations and tell lengthy stories, often mixing up fact and fiction.

She comprehends very little of the past and future, living mainly in the present. In stories she shows a limited interest in the plot itself. When she listens to stories she tends to act out what is happening in a muscular sense, assuming the bodily postures and gestures of the characters. Therefore, simple stories that have a great deal of physical action and not too much plot will appeal strongly to her at this age.

In her fourth year her drawings will not be artistic or even reasonably complete from an adult point of view, but they do show that she is paying attention to certain details. In drawing a man, she might draw a head with no body, but on the head will be two appendages that may be ears, arms, or legs. She may even draw two eyes.

A child at four tends to be a little bossy to younger children. She will probably be reasonably self-reliant in her personal habits, going to the toilet by herself with very little help, dressing, combing her hair, and brushing her teeth with little assistance.

In playing, your four-year-old will tend to truly play together with other children, rather than playing along side other children as she did earlier. She shares things more. When she does play alone, she often talks to an imaginary playmate. At this age it will be noted that she is very good at making up excuses and alibis. This shows that she is becoming conscious of a social world outside herself, of other people who have opinions and attitudes.

She may tell stories, pure fabrication, or lies, by adult standards. These stories, however, just denote her growing imagination, and we parents must be careful in gradually and intelligently making her aware of the difference between fiction and reality. Because she is so young, she cannot distinguish, at this time, between certain aspects of reality and fantasy. In line with the above, she may develop unreasonable fears of such things as the dark, certain animals, thunder and lightning, monsters. It is important that we be sympathetic and comforting to the child and attempt to reassure her about the realities of whatever she is afraid of.

Your Child's Fifth Year

Your CHILD'S fifth year marks the end of the period of early childhood. At this time, he may appear to be quite adultlike in his mannerisms and general air of sophistication. He will no longer be so dependent on parental help. He is more agile now—he skips and jumps well, and he can even balance himself on his toes for several seconds or more. He keeps better time to music when he dances. In fact, at this time he is a good pupil for dancing and physical moves.

He is more self-dependent and self-sufficient than before and understands his world and his own place in it better. Now he will probably be in kindergarten and should adjust himself to being away from home for an extended period of time.

In the home he will be more dependable and obedient, he won't dawdle as much in what he is doing, and he may show an interest in sweeping, washing, and wiping dishes. He may show a tendency to protect his younger playmates. In his speech, he shows definite evidence of politeness and tact, another indication of increasing sociability.

In simple everyday circumstances, he shows a greater variety of emotional characteristics and attitudes. He can be serious, patient, friendly, meticulous, satisfied, and pleased at his accomplishment.

He now has personal friends and may play with them in groups of two to five. At the dinner table he is very sociable and talkative, with less tendency to quarrel. He is aware of competition and exerts himself more when competing with others. In his speech there should no longer be any sign of "baby" articulation, providing the parents have not encouraged it. By this time, he has mastered many of the grammatical intricacies of the language and expresses himself in complex sentences. His vocabulary has increased by about 50 percent since the age of four.

In answering questions he is briefer and more to the point than a year earlier, and he is less inclined to ramble. Unlike in earlier periods, he asks questions to find out information he actually wants to know, not just to get your attention and hear himself talk. His questions have immediate application to the world around him. He wants to know what things are for and what they do.

He pays much more attention to details. Now he can draw a picture of a person that is recognizable. He can isolate the particular word or phrase in conversation that puzzles him rather than reacting to the statement as a whole.

He develops greater appreciation of time and the duration of events. In stories his interest turns to plot and sequence, and he can now retell a story more accurately, remembering its plot and the order of events. He may want to watch more television, and in this parental supervision is urged. (See the end of Your Child's Third Year in this chapter for a more detailed discussion of your child's television viewing habits.) Play activity will carry over from one day to the next, and he now shows a memory for remote events and places. Yesterday and tomorrow take on a definite meaning for him.

Your Child's Sixth Year

IN THE YEAR from five to six, your child will again be entering a new phase of life. This is the time when she is prone to venture farther from home unaccompanied, and if she has been allowed to gradually explore the immediate neighborhood on her own, she will generally have returned home safely and have gained confidence in her orientation to her larger environment.

She should dress herself independently except for such difficult things as tying shoelaces or, for boys, a tie. She should brush her own teeth, wash herself with little supervision, and keep her room and her personal belongings in order. She should have responsibility for such things as feeding the cat or dog, watering her own plants, and putting away her wagon or bicycle when through playing. She should now have the first introduction to using money and should be permitted to make small purchases. Through all these activities the child is developing attitudes of self-reliance, independence, and orderliness.

Individual parents will know best which small daily duties to give their child at this time. If the child is not trained to perform specific duties in this period, it may be more difficult to instill a willingness to assume and fulfill responsibilities properly later. Stories and fine examples on this topic of self-reliance and responsibility, as found in the literature of *My Book House*, will be of great help in this period.

Around the sixth year, the child tends to be less imitative of others and is becoming more of an individual. Personality characteristics become more marked and typical. Children differ as widely in personality as adults; they can vary greatly along such characteristics as activity level, persistence, distractibility, emotionality, soothability, adaptability, and extroversion or introversion. (For more information, see the section on temperament in chapter 5 of this book). Shy children should be encouraged, but not pushed, to play with others.

Group play activity typically increases around age six as the child engages in games such as hide-and-go-seek, tag, jumping rope, races, and rough-and-tumble. This form of activity and freedom makes for more noise, but it makes the child more self-reliant under competitive conditions. Another character-

istic change in play activities is that activities which had formerly occupied only a relatively short period of time now hold her attention much longer. Thus, during her sixth year your child will often play games for several hours or even over several days, continuing from the point at which she and her playmates previously left off. The child's motor skills are improving and can be seen in her progress in both table games like coloring pictures or jigsaw puzzles, as well as more active sports, such as skating. She may display a surprising degree of skill in these activities.

After her often long and active days in this period, it may be necessary to relax her so she can get her much needed rest. One of the most satisfactory and oldest methods of doing this is by telling stories. At this age the child is capable of sustaining interest in long stories; she seems to enjoy them so much that she often wants a story to be repeated on consecutive nights. Unlike the younger child, she seeks meaning in stories and pictures, and she is no longer content with merely knowing the contents of a picture. For this purpose *My Book House* is ideal since it has stories indexed according to authors, titles, leading characters, special subjects, and character traits. It is possible to illustrate by story and example not only the answers to many of the child's questions, but also such matters as proper conduct and morals, which are often difficult to communicate. Thus, the evening reading period may well become a time for gaining an understanding of your growing child, as well as guiding her development in the moral and spiritual aspects.

Your Child's Seventh, Eighth, and Ninth Years

Physical and Intellectual Growth

AFTER THE CHILD reaches his sixth birthday, his development is less well defined in terms of year-by-year growth. He is now in the "middle period" of childhood. The kinds of activities he favors are those which use large muscles, such as running, bicycling, swimming, skating, acrobatics, wrestling, and jumping. However, he also attempts highly skilled activities for which he is not quite ready. These include such acts as using tools to make airplanes or boats. The child is not ready to do these skilled acts because the finer muscle groups in his fingers are not yet fully coordinated for such use; hence, his desire often outruns his performance. But as these attempts enhance his physical development, they should be encouraged. Many toy tools, sewing kits, and the like are advertised for use at different ages. Parents should be careful to choose those games and tools which sufficiently challenge a child's abilities and yet allow him the necessary success in completing tasks.

We can now notice our child becoming less and less dependent upon us. In his behavior about the house he seems to have "grown up." At meals he is able to use a knife to spread butter or jam or cut his meat rather skillfully. You can rely on his being able to tell the correct time within a quarter hour. He bathes and goes to bed without assistance. In light of this increasing independence we see our child loosening the proverbial apron string. In his intellectual growth there has been a shift to more abstract thinking. He is better able to understand words and our answers to his questions. During this period the child becomes able to detect general similarities and differences between objects known to him, such as a baseball and an orange, an airplane and a kite. When he is told a story or a joke, he can detect the absurd elements.

During this period he begins to read on his own initiative. With an increased facility in reading, he will find greater and greater pleasure in it. He develops an ability to grasp the more difficult sentence structures and at the same time seems to enjoy the involved expressions used. During this period it is important that informative stories be made available to the child. For example, the care and feeding of pets can be learned by reading animal stories, and geographical and sociological information can be learned by reading stories about other peoples and their customs in their respective countries. The child's reading, however, should not be restricted to informative reading or reading for amusement. His reading should also include material in which he is reading for a purpose, such as following directions to build or make things. Such a varied and careful selection has already been made in *My Book House* collection. As the child learns to get the most out of his reading, he unconsciously acquires good reading habits that will aid his progress in school.

In this period we see our child seeking a place among his friends through both physical and intellectual effort. His degree of success determines his position in relation to them. Encouragement and careful background guidance for the child's many activities at this time will repay us. He should be permitted to have more freedom in his activities.

———

Your Child's Seventh, Eighth, and Ninth Years

Development of Social Behavior

As THE CHILD grows physically and mentally during the years seven to nine, he also gains in social experience. His school and extended neighborhood contacts are now giving him a much larger group of friends than he had before. Social participation on the playground, in school, and in the neighborhood is characteristic of this period. However, there is a good deal of difference among children in their social tendencies and interests. Some of them will naturally be outgoing and happy, others will appear self-centered and prefer to be left alone. A condition which may influence a child's withdrawal to solitary play is the feeling that he is not like other children physically, for instance, if he is taller, fatter, or has a physical defect. If the parents have not discussed such conditions with their child early in life, the child may have no way of compensating for these defects. In addition, if the child feels different socially, he may avoid his more fortunate playmates. Parents need to exercise much understanding and patience in dealing with their child in these circumstances, and they must stress how what really matters is not appearance but what is inside a person, whether they are a good and kind person. In addition, they may also point out that every individual has strengths and weaknesses; some are just more visible than others. Parents may also want to read your child stories and poems dealing with the themes of courage, forgiveness, kindness, and tolerance.

Between seven and nine, a child spends much of his time playing. Among friends he may like to show off, performing acts of daring, speed, or skill. He may boast about his exploits, and in order to add to this, he will often include the "great deeds" of father, mother, or older siblings. In turn, there is a brutal frankness in judging the achievements and shortcomings of playmates and those of older persons. When he is with adults, he wants to be treated as an adult. His conversation with adults may sometimes be annoying because of

his curiosity and talkativeness. This is most true when he is prying into personal affairs or monopolizing the conversation. We parents must bear with the experimenting, growing child. We can suggest other activities to him and thus frequently prevent these annoyances, but to simply suppress natural behavior may lead him to withdraw. Unsatisfactory responses from parents to his social efforts may result in his going to others to seek the information, attention, and approval he craves.

The pleasure he derives from the company of others and the opportunities it gives him to perform before an audience make him an active participant in the social events of the school, church, neighborhood, and community. These events may be dramatic plays, picnics, celebrations, or special field days. Imaginative and dramatic play are very popular.

Many children now want to go to see movies, watch television, read newspapers, and listen to music on the radio or stereo. Parents should try to exercise guidance in what their child is exposed to.

Parents by this time have spent a lot of time teaching the child the difference between right and wrong. He may, however, tend to behave in a manner that will give him the most satisfaction, regardless of whether it is right or wrong. Careful, but not too obvious guidance, and consistent behavior by parents will gradually teach him these important moral and societal rules. The kind of friends the child has outside of the home is also of great importance during this age period. In *My Book House* collection, many stories may be found that illustrate the accepted mode of behavior in various situations. Through such stories, rules for proper conduct are easily transmitted to your child in an entertaining way.

We should remember that most children in this age group have a keen sense of justice regarding their punishment. Parents should realize that their child is not willing to change a satisfying act merely because we say "don't." It is our business to suggest alternative constructive behavior. He will not like to humiliate himself by acknowledging that he should not have taken Janet's doll or taken the money that was lying on the table. But if we give him understandable explanations, he will gradually try to make up for his "misdeeds" by being good and not doing the destructive act again. There is, in spite of all modern devices in child care and training, no substitute for the good examples of parents.

Your Child's Ninth Through Twelfth Years

Physical and Intellectual Growth

T HE YEARS from nine to twelve mark a stage in your child's development between late childhood and early adolescence. Physically, educationally, and socially the child is changing, and her abilities, activities, attitudes, and interests reflect these changes. Physically, children are approaching the last stage of childhood, and during this time they may enter puberty and begin to develop secondary sex characteristics, such as pubic and underarm hair, breasts, or testes. Before puberty begins, puberty changes should be explained to them.

When your child first asks questions, as she inevitably will, about sex and procreation, you should try to answer her questions. Such answers should be suited to her stage of development and understanding. Thus, for younger children you can keep your answers very simple and concrete. The older child and adolescent, however, might seek more in-depth information and more social and emotional guidance. The discussion of sex should always treat the subject as a natural phenomenon. Above all, a secretive, emotional, shamefaced or "nice-people-don't-talk-about-such-things" approach should be avoided, since from this may ensue needless fears and inhibitions that prevent the child's best possible adjustment to life. Thus, your child will be prepared for the physical changes that come with adolescence. For parents who feel uncomfortable discussing sex with their son or daughter, the following organizations can be asked for any written materials they may have or those they would recommend to you: the Council for Sex Information and Education, founded in 1977, at 2272 Colorado Blvd., No. 122B, Los Angeles, CA 90041; or the Sex Information and Education Council of the U.S., founded in 1964, at 130 W. 42nd Street, Suite 350, New York, NY 10036, Phone: 212/819-9770.

Along with physical development, physical prowess and manual dexterity increase during this period. The child is interested in and can do stunts and various kinds of acrobatics. She develops a degree of manual dexterity which satisfactorily enables her to carry out a wide variety of skilled acts. Conspicuously absent is the bungling uncertain trial-and-error manipulation of early childhood. The child becomes increasingly interested in things which "work" or "run" and will construct these either with simple tools or by using the material of mechanical sets from which a variety of more or less "complicated" machines can be constructed. Expensive toys are not necessary, though, as children are just as thrilled about building a shack out of old boards and packing cases as they would be in having expensive lumber at hand.

In play interests and activities, competitive and cooperative play become more and more prominent. The games and sports become more complex and highly organized in response to the child's increasing skills. Further, your child is now at a stage where she can not only work with greater and more continuous effort, but also with greater foresight and perseverance in achieving her goals. During this period your child will probably show an intense interest in such outdoor activities as hiking, swimming, or skating. Indoors, card and board games are popular. Puzzles, problems, and tricks are also of great interest. Nowadays, a great deal of the child's time indoors is spent listening to the radio and watching television. For discussion of your child and television see the end of "Your Child's Third Year" in this chapter.

The outstanding avenue for intellectual development in this period is still the printed word. In school your child's reading skill has been increasing and with it her interest in reading. Instead of simple stories and folk tales, your child will now prefer stories of adventure, history, nature, travel and faraway places, and famous people and events. The outstanding selection of the world's best literature to be found in *My Book House* is particularly good in this respect. By the time she is ten, your child should be able to use an encyclopedia, a dictionary, and other reference books to find information about different subjects and words she is curious about. Her reading vocabulary (the words she can recognize and whose meaning she knows when she sees them in print) will exceed her speaking vocabulary (the words she actually uses in conversation). From this time on, progress in the knowledge of the meaning of words will come for the most part through books and literature.

Good reading habits can be fostered and built upon the natural interests of the child. There is an old saying, "Tell me your friends and I'll tell you what you are!" It is equally true that if you "tell me the books you read, I'll tell you what you are!"

The great philosopher and poet, Santayana said, "A man who gives a wrong twist to your mind, meddles with you just as truly as if they hit you in the eye; the mark may be less painful, but it's more lasting."

Your Child's Ninth through Twelfth Years

The Development of Social Behavior

BETWEEN NINE and twelve years of age, changes in social behavior stand out more than those in the physical and intellectual realms. Parents will notice a distinct change in the kinds of activities in which their child participates. The sports she plays now will put a higher premium on team play as opposed to individual play. Development in skilled performance will be along the lines of the kind of specialization which team play requires. More than mere specialization and skill, however, is involved here. In team play, the individual's talents are merged into the team somewhat, and a child may experience some degree of conflict between her desire for individual recognition and superiority, and her desire for the success of the team. Such team play will furnish the best kind of training in cooperation and sportsmanship for later life.

Hero worship manifests itself during this period. In most instances the hero is an actual person whom a child admires and tries to imitate rather than a fictional character. It may be a movie or sports star, a neighborhood "big shot," a teacher, or an admired relative. Though a child's ideals and aspirations are often short-lived during this time and follow one another in rapid succession, parents should realize the importance of this hero worship in affecting the outlook and behavior of their child. Parents should emphasize the hero's good points while pointing out some of his or her bad points.

A last important feature of this period is the manifestation of an increasing self-reliance and dependability in the child. With her new capacities comes a certain urge to independence and initiative. Your child may find ways of earning money for herself by doing odd jobs or running errands. The child, depending on the safety of the area, may be trusted to go about her hometown freely. She will make minor purchases for herself. At this time she may write occasional short letters to a vacationing friend or a relative or a teacher. She answers ads and makes purchases by mail for booklets, samples, toys, and gadgets. She makes her own telephone calls.

A child of this age often wants to be responsible for her own conduct and to make certain decisions and plans for herself. This increase in self-assertiveness is the first sign of the "declaration for independence" that typically comes with adolescence. Unless parents realize the significance of this, unless they know and are prepared to use this tendency to help their child stand on her own feet, a great deal of conflict and misunderstanding may occur. One of the difficulties is that sometimes the child compels us to treat her like an adult and at other times her immaturity and lack of experience make an outside authority necessary. This inconsistency of treatment can make things hard on both parent and child but the parent should keep in mind that while your adolescent wants a certain amount of independence, she still needs and wants you to draw firm lines in discipline and to advise her in their decisions about weighty matters like school, career choice, and interpersonal matters like friends and romantic interests.

Your Child's Twelfth to Fourteenth Years

The Early Adolescent Period

FROM TWELVE to fourteen the young boy or girl begins to change into a young man or woman. Changes in this period vary greatly among children of the same age. Tall Jack Jackson at thirteen may have acquired a deep voice and even a bit of peach fuzz on his cheek, which he is trying to cultivate, train, and coax into becoming sideburns, while his friend James, who is exactly the same age, may still have a peaches-and-cream complexion and a high-pitched young boy's voice and be a couple of inches shorter than Jack. Both parents and children should be aware that there are widely differing individual rates of growth in this period. "Normal" is not a word that finds easy application in this period.

With their developing physical maturity, girls' and boys' conception of themselves will change. Parallel with dropping their former childish preoccupations, activities, and amusements (for instance, playing with a doll is strictly passé), they may assume an adult air. Younger children in the family or neighborhood are often the first to feel and notice this change, since older children often show an attitude of condescension toward them. As adults, we will notice it, too, and it may seem exaggerated and out of character. However, we should not laugh or make fun of these signs of growing up. This is a period of change and readjustment and parents, through their treatment of and attitude toward children, can help ease their child's adjustment to the changes they are experiencing.

With girlfriends her own age, Tammy is forming a social group which is different from the spontaneous play groups of earlier periods in that membership, rather than being casual, is conscious and worked for. There are certain standards of dress and behavior that are required to fit in and "belong." One or two girls in the group may be Tammy's closer friends, and in these smaller, more intimate groups, close confidences are often exchanged.

Tammy looks to older girls for models in dress and behavior. Parents may be annoyed that their authority is disputed with a quotation of some older adolescent who is by some mysterious process presumed to have knowledge, experience, and wisdom far beyond that of parents and older people. However, we should realize that this is natural; it shows a kind of "psychological weaning." It shows that your child feels a sufficient difference of point of view and outlook from you.

During this period Tammy may begin to look at boys a bit differently. Some will no longer be seen as just playmates. They'll become interesting as examples of the opposite sex. Adolescents' mixed play, instead of being focused on the game itself like earlier periods, may now be a vehicle or means for mutual association. Thus, in games of tag there is a tendency for boys to chase girls and vice versa, rather than random or indiscriminate tagging. Lulls in activity are similarly lacking in spontaneity and are self-conscious. There is a lot of just standing around at a distance, talking, teasing, even arguing, with jibes and name-calling. Social graces and smooth talk are things of the future. Children now just grope about for something to be doing or saying, often something that covers up their lack of sophistication and lack of self-confidence.

While Tammy undergoes rather marked changes during these two years, Jack undergoes relatively slight changes. Boys, in general, mature a little later than girls. In these two years his development is extended along previously indicated lines. He is still primarily interested in his group activities, such as his band or sports. Parents should grant children of this age the greater freedom that their widened scope of activities and interests require. This is a time when individual hobbies and interests deepen, and parents should let children pursue them. All along, the "apron string" should grow less binding. For boys, the Boy Scouts may have a special appeal at this time as well as other similar organizations which take the boy outdoors. Here are provided not only the group spirit and solidarity as exemplified in pledges, laws, secret signs, and rituals, but also the organization of activity in which the child can exercise his skills and abilities, not only in competition with other individuals, but also in competition with his own past record.

In this period, boys may become more concerned about their appearance. In these matters, as the French say, "Look for the woman!" Boys become interested in girls, perhaps even a special one. Of course, they do not have the

"line" or the confident manner to single her out, but, rather, they may tease her more than the other girls or manage to be near her to hold her hand in games more often than mere chance could provide. These are the first vague manifestations of "puppy love," considered by psychologists as both necessary and very important as a basis for the later selection of a real mate.

In social gatherings, such as parties, dances, or church socials, children get their first opportunity to meet each other on a more formal footing, a preview of what high school life will be like. These contacts are attended by a great deal of self-consciousness on the part of both boys and girls. In all their social contacts children are trying to acclimate themselves to a new situation in which there are new distinctions and in which new modes of behavior are expected of them. Naturally this requires readjustment.

Indicative of this readjustment is the changed attitude in both boys and girls toward the world outside themselves. Whereas before the larger "outside" was just a convenient background for their activities, now it becomes an increasingly social world. The boy and the girl become aware of rules and regulations guiding conduct in society, and become concerned with what other people think of them. They have more regard for standards and tend toward self-analysis, self-criticism, and, surprisingly enough, self-improvement.

With this awareness of what the outside world thinks of them comes a more clear conception of themselves as individual personalities. They want their opinions and desires to be respected and given consideration. Rather than trying to repress this tendency, parents should recognize it as an important phase of growing up or of psychological weaning. We should make allowances and concessions to it in our discipline and way of thinking. Otherwise, we may either stifle this growing independence in children or else have it express itself in behavioral difficulties and open rebellion later on. While in this period we have to expect and understand a good deal of "day dreaming" through which children are trying to understand themselves and the world about them; we should also see to it that they continue to have definite routine duties within the family group.

Their growing sense of identity can be seen in their desire for privacy, for a certain corner of the house, whether it be only a bureau drawer or an entire room, which is entirely their own and to which no other member of the family has access. Parents should agree to this reasonable request. The feeling of having some rights to privacy is not a privilege, but is a necessity for growing children of this age. Parents should begin getting used to the idea that certain affairs of our children are none of our business.

Indicative of this change in viewpoint of the youngster at this age is the way in which they spend their allowance. The girl may try to corner the market on beauty preparations and return resplendent with rouge, lipstick, fingernail polish, and eyebrow pencil. Restraint is necessary on the part of the parent who first gazes upon their own sweet daughter beaming at them, expecting approval, from under her camouflage of makeup. We must remember that while your daughter looks to you like a voodoo medicine doctor in war paint, in her mirror she sees the blossoming likeness of Cleopatra, Helen of Troy, and other beauties of history. Guidance rather than repression of this tendency is the keynote in this situation.

Your young boy, rather than spending his money conservatively on school needs and candy throughout the week, may suddenly and unaccountably, even to himself , sink his entire allowance in a big pizza pie or two hot fudge butter pecan sundaes topped with whipped cream for himself and a girl. Of course, such unwise spending should not be encouraged, but special circumstances do arise in even the most well-ordered lives.

Representative, too, of children's changing outlook are their reading interests which become more diversified. The familiar, the commonplace, the near-at-hand, are no longer interesting. Books now are expected to take children out of their immediate world, to introduce them to what they have not seen or known personally, and to increase their scope of knowledge. Dramatized history, autobiography, travel, and accounts of scientific discovery have a great appeal. However, in all of these there must be sufficient action and adventure to grip the reader's interest. Action and adventure stories per se are also quite popular at this age.

Leaders are made not born.

Few children are born leaders. Whether they acquire the qualities of leadership depends upon how they learn to meet every task and problem of life—from infancy on. Your child's adult personality will be the result of his childhood experiences. The important thing is early training

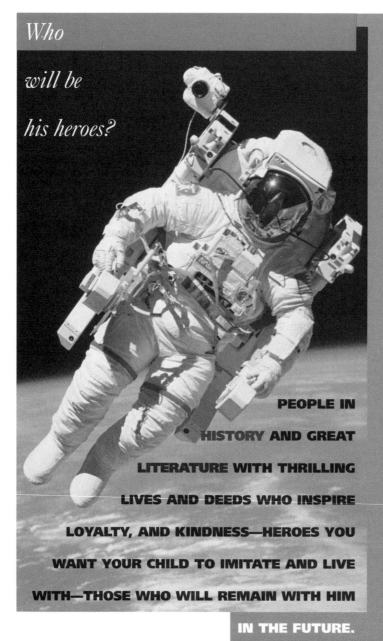

Who will be his heroes?

PEOPLE IN HISTORY AND GREAT LITERATURE WITH THRILLING LIVES AND DEEDS WHO INSPIRE LOYALTY, AND KINDNESS—HEROES YOU WANT YOUR CHILD TO IMITATE AND LIVE WITH—THOSE WHO WILL REMAIN WITH HIM IN THE FUTURE.

Characters in over stimulating and lurid movies, trashy cartoons, and other media containing all of the undesirable influences you want to neutralize when they are not avoidable.

Parents are important in encouraging the development of their children's creative ability.

17

Creative Expression in Children

Aᴌᴌ ᴄʜɪʟᴅʀᴇɴ for the sake of their own well-rounded emotional development need many opportunities to express their ideas and emotions by handling and experimenting with materials.

The child who is able to make the dreams of his imagination come true by modeling in clay, writing a story or poem, or building a model airplane will be inspired to work out his ideas again and again. Everything a child creates, no matter how crude, helps him develop confidence in his abilities to make changes in the world around him.

Let Your Child Experiment with Materials

The child does much of his thinking through handling materials. It is the parent's responsibility to see that he is free to express himself in a creative way during his early years at home. Clay, paper, chalk, crayons, paint, wood, blocks, sand, cloth, and finger paint are but a few of the materials the child can use to express his ideas in a creative manner. Something creative can be made from every material, but you may find that some will have a stronger appeal to your child than others. Your child may hesitate or even fail in his efforts to express his ideas with chalk or crayons only to discover clay or paint an excellent medium.

Encourage him to try many different materials so he can choose the ones he prefers. Let your child decide on the materials that will best express his own ideas. Show him the mere fundamentals of handling clay, give him the right size crayon and paper, and leave him to use these in his own way. Begin early to give your child a background of experiences and stories that will enrich his thinking and fire his imagination, and the urge to create will follow naturally. He should be allowed to create what he chooses—what he sees in his mind's eye—rather than be encouraged to depend on others for ideas and directions. If he learns to use clay, paint, or wood in accordance with your definite instructions, he will gain in the ability to handle the materials, but lose the opportunity to express himself in an emotionally satisfying and creative way. Your child's own crude creations will give him more satisfaction than the finest objects made by others.

Your Attitude Is Important

Parents play a very important role in encouraging and developing creative ability in the child. The parents' attitude toward their own daily work will tend to set the child's attitude for his own activities and chores. The more familiar parents are with the things that make up their child's world, the more intelligent and sympathetic will be the guidance they are able to offer. Be tolerant and understanding in your attitude toward your child's work, and you will find him exhibiting this same attitude in his criticism of the work of others.

Do not place too much emphasis on the finished objects your child has made. Be more concerned with the growth and understanding that has taken place within him while he shaped his clay hen or drew his version of an airplane he saw in the sky. The attitude you take toward your child's work will influence his further attempts at creative expression. Be enthusiastic in your praise of the things he has done well and casual in your suggestions. Try not to criticize his finished products. Encourage him to finish the job he started before he begins another, to persevere until he has learned to do the thing he started out to accomplish. Make him feel that you are happy to help him in times of difficulties. A simple suggestion about how to wipe the excess paint off his brush on the side of the paint jar may be the means of helping him overcome "runs" that are spoiling his pictures. Be sure to encourage original ideas and, at the same time, discourage thoughtless imitation. Anything that your child creates as a result of an inner experience is far more worthy of your praise than the cleverest copy of the work of others.

Help your child feel the joy of accomplishment that comes from work well done, and you will help him develop a lasting, happy, and enthusiastic attitude toward work.

Ask Your Child to Tell You

It is better to ask your child if he would like to tell you about the interesting things he is doing than to ask, "What is it?" If your child feels you do not understand what he is trying to do, he may think he has failed to do a good job. Very often his finished product will not reveal his original ideas to you. Young children let their imagination fill in the details that they are unable to work out with their hands, so it is usually best to let younger children tell you about their pictures so that you may follow their thinking and better understand their efforts.

The Child's Creative Work Is a Valuable Key to His Thinking

By carefully studying the details of your child's work you will have a valuable key to his thoughts and interests. You will be better able to interpret his emotional reactions to situations in the home and to new contacts at school and in the community. The objects your child creates will represent his sincere efforts to portray his impressions and record how well he has observed the important details of the things he has experienced. After a trip to the zoo, a child of two years will be satisfied to let a few strokes of the paint brush represent his idea of the lion's roar. Sound and action appeal to him at this age, so he may emphasize these instead of the lion's form. The child of three may attempt to paint his impression of the same lion by blotches of paint on paper, while a child of four, five, and six, may record the mane of the lion as his most outstanding impression. The six-year-old may put his picture of a lion in a cage to show his sense of caution, or add other details that reflect his maturity of thought.

Children's drawings may reveal intimate thoughts that could otherwise go unnoticed.

18

Give Your Child Crayon and Paint

Long before children are able to express ideas in words, they will attempt to portray them in crude form with paint and crayon. The pictures children draw represent their sincere efforts to record their feelings and impressions. They draw for the joy and satisfaction felt in the activity, not because they want to impress others with the results. If you examine your child's painting and drawing with this understanding, you will become familiar with some of the intimate impressions she is forming about the world around her.

As early as twelve to fifteen months, the baby may reach for the pencil or crayon she sees the adult using. If this crayon is large enough for her to grasp in her little hands, she will try pounding it on the paper in an effort to make a mark. The same baby at eighteen months will be able to use a crayon or long-handled easel brush to scribble or scrub on the paper. Younger children are primarily interested in the activity paint and crayons provide, and the sense of power they feel in their own accomplishment pleases them greatly.

Drawing and Language Ability Go Hand in Hand

In this early stage, it is interesting that children's ability to express themselves with paint and crayon will correspond closely with their power to use language. When they are in the scribble stage with their crayon or paint, they are also beginning to discard their babbling to repeat the few isolated words they are learning to say.

Two- and Three-Year-Olds

By the time they are two, you can expect them to paint one color on top of another in their pictures. Their scribblings will begin to emerge into circles and blotches, and while they sometimes name their drawings, they are more interested in the process of making them than in the results they achieve. It is not until children are past three that we can recognize what they are drawing and be certain of interpreting them correctly. For this reason, it is best to ask children to tell you about their pictures. This approach will also encourage them to use the new words they are acquiring from day to day. Do not be alarmed if the two- or three-year-old starts to tell you one thing about her picture and then, all of a sudden, changes her story. At this age and up until four, your child's imagination usually dictates the words she chooses to describe her experiences. The three-year-old enjoys moving her crayon back and forth across the paper in sweeping motions. It is a thrilling experience for them to be able to cover a piece of paper with color. A little later, she will call these strokes and blotches of color a sky, a road, or whatever her fancy dictates at the time she is making them.

Drawings of Four-Year-Olds Begin to Take on Form

Fantastic designs are popular with the young child, and they serve to represent many things. By four, children's work should begin to take on form and meaning and be more readily recognized by adults, even though it is lacking in detail. If three- or four-year-olds were to attempt to paint the elephant they have seen for the first time, their pictures would probably be little more than the trunk and a scribble. The trunk of the elephant makes a tremendous impression on children of this age. Young children prefer bold colors to express their simple, sincere beliefs. You may be sure that the color children choose to paint their elephant will be far from its natural somber gray. Four-year-olds often treasure their drawings as prized possessions.

Drawings of Five-Year-Olds Express Individuality

Five-year-olds draw with a definite idea in mind. They are familiar with the names of colors and choose them with great care. Their drawings express their freedom or restraint. Five-year-olds' drawings are truly an expression of their individuality rather than of their training. So they will readily reveal their timidity or feeling of security. At five, children try their hand at making people, houses, boats, trains, animals, and even landscapes with trees, flowers, sun, and moon. The details they consider most important will be drawn largest in their pictures. Their paints and crayons will help them express experiences they had at the zoo, circus, or airport, and you will discover they have learned many new words as they tell you the story of their pictures.

Drawing and painting give children many opportunities to develop initiative and concentration. They will put forth tremendous effort to express a happy experience and will learn to coordinate their hand and mind as they begin to think things through logically. Parents can help promote creative ability in children by developing their imagination and curiosity with a well-rounded background of age-graded literature that is colorfully illustrated. Let your child feel free to experiment with her crayons, paper, and paint. The best role for parents to play in directing the use of creative materials is that of a sympathetic shadow in the background.

Emotional Reactions Reflected

Children's drawings should take on form as they mature, and parents should be able to observe mental growth in their pictures from month to month. Children's drawings may reveal some of their intimate thoughts and impressions that would otherwise not be apparent. Their reaction to the new baby in the family, their first trip to the zoo, the parade they watched are all bound to seep into their pictures, and observant parents will be able to detect thoughts that are disturbing children's feelings of security. Drawings may also reveal their needs for understanding, encouragement, and a richer background of firsthand experiences and stories.

Children Sensitive to Beauty Around Them

Children will unconsciously formulate their ideas of color harmony and beauty from the things they see around them. They become sensitive to the color combinations they see in nature and even to the colors in their clothing and picture books. Some children are naturally more sensitive to beauty and color than others so it is a good idea to draw your child's attention to things that are particularly beautiful and attractive. When out walking, you might remark about the lovely green of the grass, the blue of the water in the lake, or the cheerful song of the robin. All these experiences will encourage an awareness and appreciation for beauty in your child. Let her help arrange the flowers for your table, decide on the color of socks or shirt that she will wear. It is through simple everyday experiences like these that the young child becomes conscious of the beauty around her. Make it a special treat to visit a flower show or the art department of your favorite store. If you are visiting the art gallery or museum, be careful not to bore her with detailed information beyond her interest and understanding.

Some simple equipment and materials that will help set the stage for the growth of free expression in your child's painting and drawing are listed below.

Painting

You may want to buy a watercolor painting set which includes a number of colors and at least one brush. Books of thick blank paper in various sizes made specifically for watercolors are also handy. Both of these items are available at art supply stores. Or you may want to obtain the more "deluxe" set of items listed below.

- Easel.
- Several long-handled brushes—about 12 inches long. A good assortment includes 1/4-, 1/2-, and 3/4-inch bristles.
- Calcimine powder paint may be purchased inexpensively at any paint store. Start with two or four colors. Red, blue, yellow, and brown are good basic colors. The powder paint can be mixed as needed.
- Empty jars that can be covered with a lid are fine for keeping the paint fresh. It is best to mix it in small quantities. One part calcimine powder to two parts water makes a satisfactory mixture. Stir the powder and water with a stick until well mixed.

- Pad of newsprint for easel—18 by 24 inches. Wrapping paper or wallpaper used on the reversed side.
- Smock or coverall for child.
- Cloth to wipe paint off brushes.
- Small wash basin and cloth for children to use to wash easel and brushes when finished painting. Thumb tacks to fasten paper to easel.
- Twine or clothesline and clothespins to hang paintings on until dry.

Drawing

- Large sheets of wrapping paper saved from packages. Pad of newsprint—18 by 24 inches—sold especially for easel drawing.
- Sheets of wrapping paper or newsprint may be pasted together for projects like friezes, wall hangings, and scenery.
- Large wax crayons—assorted colors.
- Colored chalk.
- Thick pencil.
- Charcoal.

Suggestions That Will Help Your Child Handle Paints and Crayons More Skillfully

- Place newspapers or plastic drop cloths on floor under easel before starting to paint.
- Fasten paper to easel with thumb tacks to hold it securely.
- Encourage children to use large arm movements for using crayons and painting. (Sheets of paper 18 by 24 inches, allow them more freedom to do this.)
- Wipe excess paint off brush by pressing it against the side of the jar. (This prevents runs that spoil the pictures.)
- Hang freshly painted pictures on line to dry. Wooden pinch-type clothespins will hold the paper securely and are easy for children to handle.
- Use a basin, cloth, and water to wash the easel and brushes each time they are used.
- Place lids on jars to prevent paint from drying when not in use.

Mixing Colors

Children from five to seven are ready to learn to mix their own color combinations. Let them mix red and blue and discover they have purple. Show them how to make orange by mixing red and yellow; green by mixing blue and yellow; and gray by mixing black and white.

Children like to draw and paint favorite characters and scenes from their stories. Children's pictures will express originality if we do not try to suggest patterns of conventional people or objects to them.

Friezes and posters are a favorite of children from kindergarten through high school. They may be painted or crayoned on strips of wrapping paper or newsprint. Older children may want to choose muslin or oilcloth to make a permanent frieze. This type of activity belongs to children of kindergarten age and above. As a rule, two or more children will paint on the frieze at the same time. Friezes and posters adapt themselves well to social studies in school. A frieze depicting colonial life, Indian life, and life in other lands will give children a great opportunity to record many of the interesting customs they have read about in their studies.

REFERENCES

See Creative Expression in various charts in chapter 15 of this book.
See also selections listed in index of *My Book House*, volume XII, under Artists and Illustrators, page 248.

Your child

lives in

a world

of giants

You

bridge the gap between his world

and the adult world

Holidays are times that should bring the family close together.

19

Holidays Begin at Home

YOUNG CHILDREN gather meaning of the holidays from the associations woven around them in their own home. It is difficult for them to grasp the significance of Christmas, Easter, Fourth of July, etc., unless they have a meaningful part in their celebration. Holidays should bring the family close together and provide a good time for everyone to work and plan for a happy occasion. Young children will enter into the holiday spirit if they are allowed to help make cookies, candy, and decorations for the house and table and arrange the activities of the day.

Some holidays are ones for reverence, like Christmas, Easter, and Thanksgiving, and the celebration should suit the spirit of the holiday. Others are ones of obligation and respect, and children will enter into this spirit only if the parent plants the significant thought in initial celebrations. New Year's Day, St. Valentine's Day, and Halloween are truly happy, fun-making occasions for children, and the playful spirit with which they are celebrated will enhance memories of them.

Stories and pictures help young children begin their appreciation and understanding of holidays. The story of Abraham Lincoln and the robins will give children a friendly feeling toward the great statesman. Young children will begin to build their ideas of Flag Day when they hear the story "George Washington and the First American Flag." The red, white, and blue of the flag will mean more to them when they know the names of the colors and why they were chosen. Begin with simple truths that children can understand, and add to these from time to time as they grow and mature.

Music and song will also help children capture the spirit of the holidays. Christmas carols and church bells, marches and national music, and the weird music of witches and goblins add to an intangible quality of holidays.

References

For holiday selections in *My Book House*, see index, volume XII, page 264.

Today

is but one

fleeting

moment

a miracle

that

will not

be repeated

*D*ramatic
play can help
develop initiative,
poise, originality,
and a sense of
responsibility.

20

Dramatic Play

IF YOU WANT your child to develop poise, originality, initiative, and a sense of responsibility, be sure to encourage his efforts at dramatic play. Dramatization that is free and spontaneous is natural and pleasing to the child. It gives him another outlet through which he may actively express his feelings and enthusiasm.

The tiny baby begins to imitate the actions of the people around him long before he has learned to say words. Up until three the child is unconsciously dramatizing the actions of the people around him. By the time a child is three his vocabulary is usually enough for him to try imitating the language of others as well as to express some of his own ideas. He loses himself entirely in his dramatic play and puts forth great energy in trying to be realistic. The young child learns to make many desirable social adjustments as he imitates Mom and Dad in their own daily activities.

If you place a few discarded hats, shoes, boots, a shawl, a cane, unusual hats, pants, and dresses in a box or chest for your child, he will joyously enter into simple childlike dramatic play. The young child does not need scenery to make his play-acting sincere. His imagination can quickly change the discarded party dress into the gown of a beautiful princess or the cane into a magic wand. *My Book House* will enable you to give your child the story background to awaken his interest and inspire his thinking.

In addition, dramatic play gives the "only child" and the timid child opportunities to feel the courage and confidence of the acted characters.

The Child Remembers Best What He Learns Dramatically

When a child plays an active role in doing things, he is in a sense learning how to do those things dramatically. Educators have long made use of this principle of learning, and the activity programs in schools are built around this very thought. When your first-grader tells you he is building a home, post office, firehouse, or airport at school, and your older child mentions that she is building a replica of a colonial mansion in her classroom, you will understand that these activities are planned to make their studies more interesting and meaningful. All these activities impart information to children and teach them how to work with others. In order to be a good astronaut, for example, your child must first become familiar with the duties and responsibilities of astronauts. He will seek information and stories that will tell him more about astronauts in order to excel in his role.

Dramatic play will make your child more aware of the qualities of good speech. The reading he does to gather information on each new activity will bring him in contact with many new words that he will want to use in his dramatic play.

Parents Have the Privilege of Encouraging Dramatic Play at Home

The young child enjoys acting out favorite scenes from a familiar story, and it is better to let him give his own spontaneous interpretation than to coach and rehearse him in the lines of the story. When he is old enough to feel the need for organized play-acting, let him have an active part in all the planning concerning costumes, scenery, and so forth. He is interested in dramatizing familiar nursery rhymes and parts of well-loved stories like "The Gingerbread Man," "Rama and the Tigers," or "Goldilocks and the Three Bears."

Fairy tales invite dramatization at the six- to ten-year-old level. A little later on, children will find the selections about George Washington, Abraham Lincoln, Buffalo Bill, Princess Nelly, Joan of Arc, or the Knights of the Silver

Shield more to their liking. The same fine character qualities they admire in their heroes will be reflected in their own everyday thoughts and actions. You will find stories in *My Book House* that will appeal to children at every age. The far-reaching influence of this fine background of literature will enrich your child's living every day and may lead him into many interesting hobbies.

Puppets

Puppets fascinate children of all ages. The hand puppet is easily managed by the child of five or six and will quickly take on the personality of the child operating it. Here is a pattern for a simple hand puppet that the child operates by placing thumb in one arm and third finger in the other one. The head of the puppet is operated by the index finger. The hand puppet should be made to suit the hand spread of the child who is using it. Yarn may be used for the puppet's hair; and their eyes, nose and mouth may be painted, crayoned, or sewed on with stitching or buttons. You may also wish to use clean old socks or to buy puppets.

Children under six can make puppets by cutting out pictures they have drawn on cardboard or heavy paper. These figures may be nailed or glued on a stick and used as stick puppets.

Older children will be able to think of other materials from which to construct puppets. Their imagination will suggest costume ideas for favorite story characters.

The size of the puppets will depend upon the age of the child using them and the size of the stage. Large puppets, about fifteen or sixteen inches tall, are best for the young children, as they bring the child's big hand muscles into play.

Children from fourth grade through high school will get a great deal of pleasure from making their own puppet shows. Puppet plays inspire designing costumes and scenery to fit the period and nationality of the characters. Puppet enthusiasts can read widely in the field in literature, history, and art to find the information they need to make their puppets authentic in every detail.

The puppet stage may be a simple wooden box with muslin curtains or an elaborate theater, depending on the maturity of the child making and using it. Younger children will operate their stick puppets from below the floor level of the puppet theater, while older children may want to learn to operate string puppets from the space at the top of the stage.

Puppets provide children with another avenue of expression and help them see the need for clear speech. They also help develop children's personalities. Many children who would otherwise hesitate to perform before a group seem to find the confidence to express themselves freely through the puppet characterization.

Shadow Plays

Shadow plays may be simple or complex according to the age and interests of children taking part in them.

A screen is required to produce shadow plays. A sheet, a transparent window shade, or a movie screen will serve the purpose. The size of the screen will depend on the size of the silhouettes used for the characters in the play. If you want to give human shadow plays, the screen must be large enough to reflect the child's silhouette.

The screen may be hung over a doorway or put on a roller to be raised and lowered when needed. The space at the bottom of the screen should be covered with heavy material or cardboard. Place the cardboard high enough so that the "actor" will be concealed from the audience as he manipulates the puppet. Place an electric light behind the screen to reflect the silhouette of the actor or puppet as they come between the light and the screen.

Young children enjoy using the shadow screen to act out nursery rhymes in pantomime. They get pleasure out of seeing children and adults make animal shadow pictures with their arms, hands, and fingers. Children under six can make simple cardboard figures of story characters to use in their shadow plays.

Shadow plays offer children unlimited possibilities for creative expression in writing plays and the making and designing of scenery and costumes.

REFERENCES

A number of selections in *My Book House* can be used to encourage imitation and dramatic play in your child

SUGGESTIONS FOR THE YOUNG CHILD

* "Pat-a-Cake, Pat-a-Cake, Baker's Man!" volume I, page 19
* "This Little Pig Went to Market", volume I, page 19
* "Hickory, Dickory, Dock!" volume I, page 22
* "Hippety Hop to the Barber Shop", volume I, page 28
* "Baa, Baa, Black Sheep", volume I, page 29
* "Little Bo-Peep", volume I, page 32
* "Here Am I, Little Jumping Joan", volume I, page 32
* "Little Boy Blue", volume I, page 33
* "Jack, Be Nimble", volume I, page 39
* "Jack and Jill", volume I, page 40
* "Little Miss Muffet", volume I, page 40
* "Humpty Dumpty", volume I, page 46
* "Pease-Porridge Hot", volume I, page 47
* "Little Jack Horner", volume I, page 48
* "Hop, Mother Annika!" volume I, page 74
* "Peekaboo, I See You", volume I, page 74
* "Quaker, Quaker, How Is Thee?" volume I, page 82
* "Here's the Church", volume I, page 83
* "Ring Around the Rosy", volume I, page 84
* "Teddy Bear, Teddy Bear", volume I, page 91
* "The Farmer in the Dell", volume I, page 102
* "The Barnyard", volume I, page 114
* "At the Wedding of Miss Jenny Wren", volume I, page 125
* "Monkeys", volume I, page 142
* "What Are You Able to Build With Your Blocks?", volume I, page 164
* "Good Morning, Peter", volume I, page 165
* "The Little Girl and the New Dress", volume I, page 168
* "Big Bus, Stop!" volume I, page 173
* "Policeman Joe", volume I, page 173
* "Biting Marion", volume I, page 174
* "The Three Trucks", volume I, page 177
* "The Big Engine", volume I, page 179
* "Groceries", volume I, page 182
* "Mister Postman", volume I, page 182
* "The Elevator", volume I, page 183
* "The Zoo in the Park", volume I, page 186

* "The Orchestra", volume I, page 187
* "Sally's Blue Ball", volume I, page 188
* "Park Play", volume I, page 189
* "The Big Umbrella and the Little Rubbers", volume I, page 190
* "The Snow Man", volume I, page 192
* "White Fields", volume I, page 193
* "The Little Pig", volume I, page 198
* "A Story of the Wind", volume I, page 200
* "What They Say", volume I, page 207
* "Mary and the Christ Child", volume I, page 218
* "The Little Red Hen and the Great Grain of Wheat", volume II, page 3
* "The Little Gray Pony", volume II, page 17
* "Little Gustava", volume II, page 30
* "Moon, So Round and Yellow", volume II, page 40
* "Two Birds and Their Nest", volume II, page 45
* "Johnny and the Three Goats", volume II, page 47
* "The Teddy Bears' Picnic", volume II, page 57
* "The Gingerbread Man", volume II, page 58
* "The Star", volume II, page 83
* "The Little Rabbit Who Wanted Red Wings", volume II, page 87
* "Ten Little Indians", volume II, page 94
* "Shingebiss", volume II, page 96
* "The Hare and the Tortoise", volume II, page 106
* "The Lion and The Mouse", volume II, page 108
* "The Tale of Peter Rabbit", volume II, page 112
* "Rama and the Tigers", volume II, page 118
* "Two Children", volume II, page 138
* "Paper Boats", volume II, page 139
* "The Sheep and the Pig That Made a Home", volume II, page 145
* "Late", volume II, page 153
* "Jack Frost", volume II, page 186
* "The Cock, the Mouse, and the Little Red Hen", volume II, page 192
* "The Little Engine That Could", volume II, page 200
* "Snow", volume II, page 208
* "The Night Before Christmas", volume II, page 213
* "Goldilocks and the Three Bears", volume III, page 20
* "The Brownies in The Toy Shop", volume III, page 40
* "The Circus Parade", volume III, page 46
* "Indian Children", volume III, page 94
* "The Shoemaker and the Elves", volume III, page 95
* "The Story of Li'l' Hannibal", volume III, page 116
* "Mrs. Tabby Gray", volume III, page 129

* "Of a Tailor and a Bear", volume III, page 134
* "The Shaking of the Pear Tree", volume III, page 146
* "A Happy Day in the City", volume III, page 181
* "The Wind and the Sun", volume III, page 196
* "Little Blue Apron", volume III, page 210
* "Cinderella", volume IV, page 12
* "The Selfish Giant", volume IV, page 50
* "The Boy Hero of Harlem", volume IV, page 57
* "The Battle of the Frogs and Mice", volume IV, page 104
* "Tippity Witchit's Hallowe'en", volume IV, page 145

SUGGESTIONS FOR THE OLDER CHILD

* "Hansel and Grethel", volume IV, page 73
* "The Story of Big Paul Bunyan", volume IV, page 161
* "Old Stormalong", volume IV, page 183
* "Pecos Bill, the Cowboy", volume IV, page 195
* "Jack and the Beanstalk", volume V, page 20
* "Dick Whittington and His Cat", volume V, page 33
* "George Washington and the First American Flag", volume V, page 118
* "A Story About Abe Lincoln", volume V, page 133
* "The Nuremberg Stove", volume V, page 162
* "A Midsummer Night's Dream", volume VI, page 38
* "The Wizard of Oz", volume VI, page 62
* "The Twelve Months", volume VI, page 71
* "The Three Wishes", volume VI, page 92
* "Jasper, the Drummin' Boy", volume VI, page 108
* "The Lost Spear", volume VI, page 132
* "The Boy Who Saved the World", volume VI, page 170
* "The King's Cream", volume VI, page 209
* "Rhodopis and Her Gilded Sandals", volume VII, page 84
* "Vladimir's Adventures in Search of a Fortune", volume VII, page 102
* "The Knights of the Silver Shield", volume VI, page 173
* "The Golden Touch", volume VI, page 210
* "Gulliver's Travels to Lilliput", volume VII, page 38
* "The Magic Horse", volume VIII, page 92
* "Maggie Tulliver Goes to Live With the Gypsies", volume VIII, page 189
* "Buffalo Bill", volume IX, page 27
* "Princess Nelly and the Seneca Chief", volume IX, page 78
* "The Rose and the Ring", volume IX, page 177
* "The Legend of William Tell", volume X, page 44
* "Joan of Arc", volume X, page 98

* "The Story of the Cid", volume X, page 108
* "As You Like It", volume X, page 165
* "Ye Merry Doings of Robin Hood", volume XI, page 49
* "The Melting Pot", volume XI, page 173
* "Down by the River Avon", volume XII, page 15
* "Life in Concord", volume XII, page 122

For additional references in *My Book House*, see index, volume XII—Games and Rhythms, page 263; Puppets and Shadow Plays, page 283.

Your child's mind is like film in a camera. . . it captures only that to which it is exposed

Music can help your child express many of his feelings—it truly is called the "universal language."

21

Let Your Child Discover the Joy of Music

CHILDREN ARE NEVER too young to hear good music—even infants show signs of enjoying beautiful lullabies softly crooned and played. Music should be a part of your child's daily experience, for the rhythm and sound are more basic and primitive than language itself. Babies possess a sense of rhythm from birth. They sense it in the actions of others and express it in their own bodily movements. Music reflects the moods and feelings of humanity—it is, indeed, the "universal language."

Children discover music by hearing it. Children learn to sing, as they learn to talk, through listening and imitating. Music helps your children express their thoughts and feelings—they should be encouraged to sing and express themselves rhythmically for the sheer joy it affords them.

Children Express Rhythm in Many Ways

They express it in bodily movements, words, and tunes. By eighteen months babies hum spontaneously or sing syllables in a rhythmic manner. They are alert to sounds. By twenty-four months they can usually sing a phrase of song

they have heard, although it is not always on pitch. Children of this age love a rocking horse or a rocking chair, and somehow these rocking movements seem to inspire them to express themselves in song and rhythm. They may seek ways to express their feeling of rhythm through such bodily movement as nodding their head, swinging their arms, tapping their feet, or by going around bending their knees in a bouncing motion.

Be sure that the songs and music your child hears are suitable for his impressionable mind. The melodies and poetry should be of the best, and the thought and meaning should be understandable to the individual child's level of understanding.

Many Ways to Introduce Song in the Young Child's Day

By three the child is ready to match simple tones. When parents call him they can sing his name. He may in turn imitate the parent's tune with "I'm here!"

The three-year-old can generally sing short songs, although again he may not always be on pitch. He enjoys experimenting with musical instruments and can walk, run, gallop, and jump to music in fairly good time.

The child of four is interested in dramatizing songs and enjoys "singing games" like, "Ring Around the Rosy," "The Farmer in the Dell," and "Lazy Old Mary." A child at this age often finds delight in teasing other children by singing nicknames or chants similar to, "cry baby, cry baby," or "Georgie has a girl." For more ideas, see the selections listed under Games and Rhythms in *My Book House* index, volume XII, page 263.

By five a child is ready to sing a melody on pitch and to recognize and appreciate a number of songs and tunes. He can skip with music, hop on one foot, and dance rhythmically. By listening he discovers that music can be loud or soft, fast or slow.

Homemade Instruments

Rhythm sticks, musical comb, tom-tom, rattle, or a scale of glasses tuned with varying amounts of water are a means of introducing your child to rhythm and music. The soft tone of the homemade tom-tom is far more suitable to his thin voice than the sound of an expensive commercial drum. A homemade xylophone or scale of spoons will interest children and encourage them to make up simple tunes of their own for their favorite rhymes and poems. Children enjoy hearing and examining instruments played by others. They like to imitate the motions used in playing these instruments and supply their own sound effects.

Music Can Play an Important Part in Children's Lives

Movies and radios have brought a great diversity of music within the reach of every family. The time to gain formal music training varies with individual children and depends largely on their muscular development and desire to acquire the necessary skill. However, children who are familiar with good music will have a greater incentive to persevere and practice until they have learned to play the instrument that appeals to them. Good music in the home will help reveal any inherent musical talent your child may possess. During his early years expose your child to good music and opportunities to express himself in a rhythmic fashion.

Stories of musical compositions will add to children's interest and appreciation of music. *My Book House* has included a background of lullabies, folk songs, and stories of musical composers and their compositions to help you stimulate the love for good music in your child. In the index, volume XII, on page 267 under Music, you will find many musical tales from other lands. The story illustrations show the characters in their native costumes and add color and meaning to the music your child hears.

There are many fine recordings made especially for children. To discover some of these, talk to other parents, visit music stores and ask clerks about the best and most popular ones, and check out your local public library.

Music will help your child form the habit of listening. Through listening he discovers music may be loud or soft, high or low, graceful or sturdy, and these details help him interpret the thought and mood of the song. When he has learned this, he will readily understand why he must listen and let the music talk. Music will do much to give your child freedom, joy, and happiness. If he is able to feel the freedom of song and expression, he will have a better appreciation of the beauty around him and grow in emotional poise and satisfaction.

REFERENCES

See Music in various charts in chapter 15 of this book.
See selections under Music in index of *My Book House*, volume XII, page 267.

What

lies

ahead?

A child learns good manners by imitating his parents and others around him.

22

Good Manners

THE SAYING "Good manners are good morals" reflects the fact that good manners are based upon courtesy and consideration of others. When everyday good manners become as natural to us as walking, we can easily learn the surface forms of etiquette which make us acceptable to various societies and which differ with geographical locations and customs. Manners must be learned, and children learn by imitating and absorbing the manners practiced by their mother and father and the other people around them.

It Is Never Too Early to Begin Teaching Children Manners.

The tone of voice you use to your baby forms a constant note in her early life. Cheerful voices bring cheerful responses. Long before your baby is one year old, the way you say, "I'm sorry," if you accidentally bump her becomes a keynote for her lifetime manners. Many people forget to be polite to a baby, but there is no one who learns more readily the meaning of "please" and "thank you." If you take something away from her, say, "Thank you," and give her another object to hold. Soon your smile and your "thank you" will be all that is needed to satisfy her when she gives up the object you do not want her to have.

As your child begins to walk and talk, your work is doubled. You not only have to carry on your own household duties, but must also see that this small piece of perpetual motion does not harm herself or acquire bad habits. She wants to go everywhere and to get everything into her own hands. It is her way of exploring and conquering her new world. But since she cannot be allowed to go everywhere and reach everything, you will have to be constantly on guard, checking, restraining, and diverting her. The manners you use in guiding her now will be reflected later. Considerations of a baby's needs and growing personality become your guide. Her curiosity must not be stifled with constant nagging and sharp reprimands of "Naughty, naughty" and "Don't do that." Her interests must be turned into constructive channels. To do this takes patience and knowledge of a child's way. Give her the right things to play with. Play with her yourself as much as you can. Talk to her cheerfully, no matter what work you are doing. Laugh with her. Enjoy her new-found world with her. And always respect her rights. If she is absorbed with her blocks or some activity, don't pick her up unexpectedly. Talk to her politely first, tell her what the next move is going to be. Give her time to make an adjustment. It takes only a few moments longer, and your consideration will be repaid hundreds of times in the years to come as you see her respect your rights and make considerate gestures toward others.

You will spend many hours every day with your growing baby, and every minute of every hour she will be learning your ways. She may not understand the words you say, but she soon knows the tone of happiness or anger or sadness in your voice. She knows when you say something pleasantly but firmly and when you can be coaxed into changing your mind. She also knows when you are being genuinely thoughtful and when your politeness is only a mask for other feelings. This is the time when you lay the foundation for all good manners. This is the time when you can assure her of the love and security and gentleness and warmth which will help her to grow into a healthy, happy, and responsive child. You will have no problems in teaching your child good manners when she is confident of your love and concern for her.

Every Day Brings Its Own Problems of Manners

The teaching of manners to a young child is often complicated by the manners of other children and adults. If you have lived alone with your child, you might never have any trouble. But when the child begins to play with others and when children and grown-ups come together, every parent faces difficult moments. Relatives might expect your child to behave in a certain way. On that particular day, your child may act as if she had never had a moment of training and as if you had never spent a second being courteous to her. Naturally, you are embarrassed. You feel that your child's manners are a reflection on you, and you may punish or scold her as a reaction to your own feeling of disgrace. But this is the time to stand by your child courageously and not to blame her unfairly before she has grown into full understanding of the things she does. You need not approve of her poor manners, but you must not let her feel that you've turned against her. Children are not small adults. They do many things for reasons we do not fully understand, and they seldom mean to be rude or to cause trouble. They need many years to develop mentally and emotionally as well as physically. They mature best when they feel your steady confidence in them no matter how many mistakes they make. If you make too much fuss, they feel cut off from your love.

Many Times Good Manners Mean Sharing

But young children have not discovered the pleasures of sharing their possessions. If forced to share things which they feel are their own, they may become very upset and fight back or cry loudly. A difficult time for parents of one- and two-year-olds may come when friends come by bringing their own child of that age. At such times an afternoon can turn out to be anything but friendly and peaceful. The child who has learned to let you take things from her with a smile, may scream violently as her young visitor picks up a toy. "Mine!" she bellows, clutching the toy. The visitor begins to howl and is picked up by his parent who soothes and comforts him with baby talk while your guest watches to see you scold your "selfish" child. The manners you yourself show in these crises are the manners your own child will one day imitate.

Children are not being selfish when they cling to their own things. They are being normal and natural. It will take much careful guidance which is not confused by cross words and punishments before they enjoy sharing. Try holding your child's hand and offering the young guest another toy. "Let's give Mason this horse to play with," you say cheerfully. Mason may keep up his wailing for the first toy and refuse to accept the horse. Your child may not

appear to join you graciously. But you will do something else to divert both young ones, and, later, your child will recall the friendly clasp of your hand and realize that you were trying to show her a better way of doing things. You did not desert her. You did not join the guest in snatching the toy she believed belonged to her. Before long you will be rewarded by seeing her share their toys of her own free will, using your happy tone of voice as she talks to other children.

It is important to remember that your child will not always use her new manners at the time you wish she would. If you do not let your emotions confuse her, you will be able to encourage her to try again.

Respect for Other People's Property Is a Basic Rule of Good Manners

It takes time for children to learn this rule. For example, young children love to explore women's purses. In a flash your child may seize a guest's purse and dump its contents on the floor. Or, unobserved, she may have opened the purse and used the lipstick to decorate everything in sight. Your guest is annoyed and you are upset, but this is a time when you must recognize that a purse is simply a wonderful toy to young children. It holds fascinating things from keys to mirrors and glasses. It's fun to take things out and put them back. Moreover, the child has a sense of imitating her mother when she plays with a purse. Naturally, you can't let her get into the habit of taking other people's things (though some parents allow children to do anything they please with a guest's property, thereby showing their own bad manners); but you can teach her about personal property by giving her one of your old purses to keep as her own. Fill it with keys on a ring, a mirror and an empty lipstick case. When she is tempted to take someone else's bag, insist that she get her own, and point out pleasantly, "This purse belongs to Mrs. Green. That one is yours."

It's Rude to Whine and Nag and Interrupt Another's Conversation

Yet some children learn to make a dreadful nuisance of themselves in order to get attention. They learn to know exactly what will embarrass their parents the most when others are around. They are even willing to suffer punishment if they succeed in attracting attention. There is a bigger problem than bad manners to consider if a child continues this habit. There may be something wrong in her adjustment to the world.

Parents may be at fault. Perhaps they have been so busy with their own affairs that they have failed to give a child enough attention. Perhaps parents have failed to be firm in their attitudes toward the child so that she is uncertain about the best way to behave. A child often feels insecure in her relation to her parents and feels a desperate need to attract their attention. This condition can be remedied by both parents taking time to play with her, to go on little trips about town with her and give her her own individual attention for a while. This may be all that is needed to restore harmony and put the question of manners back on a natural basis.

Watch a parent whose child interrupts her conversation. Does she give in immediately? Does she ignore the child completely? Does she snap and scold? Or does she hold out a friendly hand to detain the child until she finishes a sentence and then says, "Now I will talk to you"? Or does the parent pause and say pleasantly but firmly, "Mom (or Dad) is talking to someone. In a minute I will talk to you"? And then, does the parent keep his promise? Parents have a way of talking so steadily that a child cannot possibly get a word in. The child may feel badly left out and simply want to join in the conversation, or she may really want to know something.

Since the old rule that "children must be seen and not heard" is no longer considered a healthy idea, we must give children a chance to be part of our lives. And if good manners are based on consideration for others, we must consider children's feelings when we mix children and grown-ups. If we promise to talk to them "in a minute" we must keep that promise. If, in turn, they talk too long, we can say, "Now I must have a turn to talk to my friend." *Our own good manners give children confidence and make them want to show good manners in turn.* There are times when it is difficult to let children feel part of a group. In such a situation, we can try to give them something interesting to do while we talk to others. We can promise them companionship as soon as the other adult has gone. We can make them feel that we are thinking of their pleasure as well as our own.

Good Manners Mean Taking Turns and Playing Together

The learning of good manners is sped up for three- to six-year-olds who are beginning to play regularly with others. A group of children in a preschool or in some backyard must take turns on swings, slides, and tricycles. They must learn to wait in line to walk on an inclined plank or to climb on bars or swing in a swing. But there must be constant and friendly guidance from an adult, for some children are slower in learning than others. Some children continue to think that everything is "mine" and refuse to share with others. Teachers and parents have to cooperate in teaching such children group manners. They must be directed into satisfying play activities and discover that it's fun to share and take one's turn. Punishments and harsh words may create nothing but an added desire to smash and bother things.

Parents themselves must have good group manners. Many times, in settling trouble between children, parents begin to be rude to each other, and children soon adopt the bad manners. If neighbors are criticized at home, children will return to the playground saying, "My mother doesn't like you because . . . ," and trouble moves on in a never-ending circle.

Children under six love to play house and store and to mimic the adult world they see every day. They use the tones of voice and the very words they have heard parents use to shopkeepers, friends, and visitors. But they also express many special feelings of their own which are hard for adults to understand. For instance, a mild and charming little girl whose mother had always treated her with gentleness and respect may suddenly bang her doll's head on the floor and shout, "There, you bad, bad doll. You're naughty and bad." Any mother would be horrified and rush in to reprove her child for treating a doll so rudely. But psychologists who have spent years observing children at play advise us to turn our eyes away and put our hands over our ears at this time. The little girl is not imitating her mother but is probably working out some issue. She will probably be her own sweet self the next moment, singing a lullaby to her doll.

Good Manners Are Practiced at Home

All manners are based on consideration of others, and we all know that we first want to be considerate to those we love best. From the time we get up in the morning until we fall asleep at night, there are many chances to show consideration. In dozens of little ways we use our good manners to make living with others easier and more pleasant.

When we get up in the morning, we say a cheerful good morning to everyone. We know that a day starts off better with pleasant words. Some people have a harder time feeling awake in the morning than others and should not be expected to talk as brightly and continuously. It's not considerate to tease such children or to call them "sleepyhead" or to rumple their hair as you pass them. Let everyone be themselves.

In the matter of good table manners children must not be allowed to think that they can do as they please at home and carry another set of manners with them when they go out. Manners become second nature, and many people have been greatly embarrassed to find themselves using crude table manners in public. "No elbows on the table." "No talking with your mouth full." "No gulping water or milk and choking." "No spilling." "No playing with the silver." "No wiping your mouth with the back of your hand." There are dozens of little rules like these, about which parents constantly have to remind children. Yet it isn't the rule but the idea behind the rule which will make children want to practice it. We practice good table manners because it is considerate of others to do so. We carry on a pleasant conversation at the table, talking about interesting things we've seen and done, because this is one of the rare times a family can be together. Again, it takes patience for a parent to help their child through the period of learning good table manners. Some parents do not allow a young child to eat with adults until they have learned good manners, but most parents know that children learn quickly from example.

Children from five to eight like to be assigned small tasks, such as taking dishes to the kitchen and helping wash them. They like to please and "do things right." But their ability is limited. Don't expect them to be perfect, and always remember to praise them and thank them.

Parents can make it much easier for everyone to practice good manners by arranging a home so that everyone has a place for their own things. Some homes are arranged for adult comfort only, and there is little place for children to play or have their things. Some families let children take over the home and turn the entire place into confusion. The best homes are balanced ones. Parents may want one room which stays cleaned up, an attractive place to sit and read or entertain guests. Children need a play area where they aren't required to keep things picked up every minute.

When out in public, children must use all the good manners they have practiced at home. They must learn to meet people well, to introduce people to one another, and to accept introductions. Grownups should always introduce their child. "I want you to know my son, Justin." Don't ruffle his hair and call him pet names which might embarrass him.

We set a good example for our children by standing quietly in line without pushing or shoving when buying tickets for the movies, waiting for the cashier in a store, or waiting to pay our fare on a bus. Parents who pay no fare for young children hold them on their laps if a bus is crowded. Children often enjoy giving their seats to an elderly person or to someone with a physical disability.

Well-mannered children know instinctively how to treat individuals who are different from them. They do not speak of, or in any way call attention to, others' disabilities. They do not stare. They do not ask questions about a person's private business. They do not call names and mock others, whether they are in school, walking down the street, playing games, going to meetings, or entertaining guests in their own home. They respect everyone as an individual.

Help children to feel that manners are the gracious ways which make others admire us; that they are the oil for the machinery of daily living with others, making us feel like the finest human beings.

In teaching manners to children, parents need many years of patience and a broad understanding of the way children grow. Too often they expect children to be grown up beyond their years. Children need time, they can't be forced to grow. All the nagging, sarcasm, and punishment in the world won't turn them into polite, capable, and talented adults before their time. They can even be prevented from learning well if they are forced to act in ways too advanced for their age. Parents must be wise and sensitive in knowing how much responsibility children are ready to accept at each age. If they are pushed too hard, they will only develop unhappy traits which will keep them from getting on well at school or with other people.

Children need constant affection, reassurance, encouragement, and praise and endless gentle, nonblaming reminders if we want them to grow into well-mannered, successful, and happy human beings.

Contacts with good literature can strengthen positive character traits, good attitudes and fine ideals.

23

Character Building Index of *My Book House*— A Guide for Parents

THE ESSENTIAL purposes of the *My Book House Plan* are to introduce children to the vast storehouse of existing good literature and provide them with stimulation to promote sound character development. Through contacts with the fine literature found in *My Book House*, positive character traits, fine ideals, and healthy attitudes may be strengthened. Of course, there is no substitute for adequate training through firsthand experience, but what is read to the child and, later, what he reads himself, can be very helpful as a supplement to life experience. The Character Building Index in volume XII of *My Book House* has been designed to provide a guide for using the wide variety of material in *My Book House*. It is designed to aid your efforts to guide your child's character growth.

It is a well-known fact that children imitate what they see and hear, especially when they admire the person who is setting the pattern. The child primarily imitates those with whom he lives—especially his parents—but he also imitates characters and situations in the stories he reads and hears. It is important that he have good role models, and the collection of literature in *My Book House* provides a wealth of these.

For successful results, a story must combine interest, suitability, and literary merit. The story that preaches or moralizes fails to impress the child, and the too obvious use of a story to teach a lesson also fails. Stories should be allowed to make their own impression. The main thing is that the story, rhyme, or poem fit the child's present level of understanding. The brave little duck Shingebiss may be admired by the young child who, a few years later, may make Sir Roland his hero.

The listings in the Character Building Index (volume XII of *My Book House*) suggest links between stories and character traits such as kindness or honesty. Of course, no parent would believe that just reading a story related to a certain virtue could automatically produce that virtue in the child. Stories, along with careful management of the child's life situations, however, can help develop the qualities you wish to foster. This is particularly true in the child's early years when he is more impressionable and many of his attitudes and concepts are being formed.

The material in *My Book House* was chosen with this in mind and is carefully age-graded to fit the child's needs from infancy through adolescence. By following the progressive order of volumes, you can feel sure you have the appropriate material to supplement your other guidance efforts. It is good to let the child's individual attention span, interest, and response guide his rate of progress from the beginning volumes into the more advanced materials. The child's character and personality are built daily—on the installment plan.

A *little fellow* follows me

A careful man I want to be,
A little fellow follows me;
I do not dare to go astray,
For fear he'll go the self-same way.

I cannot once escape his eyes,
Whate'er he see me do, he tries;
Like me he says he's going to be,
The little chap who follows me.

He thinks that I am good and fine,
Believes in every word of mine;
The base in me he must not see,
The little chap who follows me.

I must remember as I go,
Through summer's sun and winter's snow;
I am building for the years to be
That little chap who follows me.

Acknowledgments
The following publishers have generously given permission to use portions of copyrighted works. From *Begin Here: The Forgotten Conditions of Teaching and Learning*, by Jacques Barzun. Copyright 1991 by The University of Chicago. Reprinted by permission of The University of Chicago Press. From *Read to Me: Raising Kids Who Love to Read*, by Bernice E. Cullinan. Copyright 1992 by Bernice E. Cullinan. Reprinted by permission of Scholastic Inc.

Photo Credits
Corbis: Morton Beebe-S.F., p. 178; Laura Dwight, pp. 16, 24, 38, 56, 126; Owen Franken, p. 12; Jeffry W. Myers, 86; Phil Schermeister, p. 7; Karl Weatherly, p. 72; David Wells, p. 162; Jennie Woodcock; Reflections Photolibrary, 188, 198; Michael S. Yamashita, p. 98.
Comstock: Comstock, Inc, 2, 8, 10, 28, 60, 68, 78, 94, 102, 156, 166, 174, 190
PhotoDisk: PhotoDisk © 1997, pp. ii, iv, 4, 22, 47, 48, 84, 125, 136, 143, 147, 159, 160, 173, 177, 187, 193, 194, 204.
The Image Works: Bob Daemmrich, p. 97
Third Coast: © John & Guy Productions/Third Coast 1997. p. 77
WestLight: © L. White/Westlight, p. vi; © R. W. Jones/Westlight, p. 55; © R.Clevinger/Westlight, p. 66; © S. Chenn/Westlight, p. 67; © W. Hodges/Westlight, p. 207